To the women of
Apartment Search,

With best regards,
Anne Glaser
April, 2000

When Money Isn't Enough

When Money Isn't Enough

HOW WOMEN ARE FINDING THE SOUL OF SUCCESS

CONNIE GLASER
AND BARBARA SMALLEY

WARNER BOOKS

A Time Warner Company

To the many women we've met who are following
their hearts and redefining success on their own.
Thank you for your inspiration.

Warner Books, Inc., 1271 Avenue of the Americas, New York, NY 10020
Visit our Web site at http://warnerbooks.com

 A Time Warner Company

Printed in the United States of America
First Printing: April 1999
10 9 8 7 6 5 4 3 2 1

Library of Congress Cataloging-in-Publication Data

Glaser, Connie Brown.
    When money isn't enough / how women are finding the
soul of success / Connie Brown Glaser and Barbara
Steinberg Smalley.
        p.   cm.
    Includes bibliographical references.
    ISBN 0-446-52303-8
    1. Women executives.   2. Businesswomen.   3. Success
in business.   4. Success.   I. Smalley, Barbara
Steinberg.   II. Title.
HD6054.3.G58   1999
650.1'082'0973—dc21   98-35790
                                                      CIP

Copyright Acknowledgments

The authors and publisher gratefully acknowledge permission to reprint the following material:

List of "The 100 Best Companies for Working Mothers" first appeared in WORK-
ING MOTHER, October 1998. Reprinted with the permission of MacDonald Com-
munications Corporation. Copyright © 1998 by MacDonald Communications
Corporation.

Selected lyrics from "I Am Woman" used by permission of Helen Reddy.

Book design by Giorgetta Bell McRee

Contents

SECTION ONE
Looking for Success in All the Wrong Places

SECTION TWO
Rewards Beyond the Bottom Line: Tales of Women Who Are Redefining Success on Their Own Terms

CONTENTS

SECTION THREE
Finding Solutions for
Work-Life Conflicts

Acknowledgments

Writing a book is a collaborative effort. In this, our third book together, we have grown to respect one another's strengths and talents more than ever. What began as a friendship ten years ago has evolved into a creative partnership, based on mutual admiration and trust.

Yet this book would never have come into being were it not for several people who believed in us and the story we felt needed to be told. Sincere thanks to our editors, Colleen Kapklein and Amy Einhorn, who identified with the book's theme and shared our passion for its message. To Jamie Raab, our publisher, who believed in the book's importance from the beginning. Heide Lange, our agent, who played a key role in the development of this book. We have come to rely on her keen insight and unfaltering good judgment in every situation we encounter. And special thanks to Larry Kirshbaum, whose continued interest and support make him our personal Man for all Reasons.

On a personal level, there were many friends and colleagues who lent us support and encouragement and helped us to see the lighter side of things while writing this book. Many thanks to Carol and Bob Deutsch and Sharon and Freddy Loef, as well as to Sandi Beals, Jenny Beznosova, Cathy Carrabis, Dr. Arthur and Lois Cohen, Beverly Cutler, Louann Cutler, Irene Daria, JoAnne Donner, Abe and Eileen Glaser, Judy and Dan Hees, Marty Johnston, Betsy Kellman, Krys Keller, Jeff and Patty Kukes, Meryl and Richard Levitt, Carrie and Ron Ludwig, Rebecca Maddox, Dr. Kathleen McCarroll, Virginia Means, Bonnie Michaels, Diane Morefield, Vicky Nikiforov, Helayne O'Keiff, Barbara Pagano, Sue Rains, Morene Seldes-Marcus, Arnold Shapiro, Levi Smith, Marcia Stamell, Gail and Kim Stearman, Melissa Wahl, Tom and Lenora White, and Susan Zalkind.

And to our siblings, who inadvertently helped us develop the tact and diplomacy that only middle children can know. To Barbara Berlin, Richard Brown, Avra Hawkins, and Dale Steinberg, thanks for always being there for us.

We are especially grateful to our families, who helped us maintain a sense of quality and balance in our lives throughout this project. Our heartfelt thanks to our wonderful husbands, Tom and Tim, and our children, Rusty and Max, Logan and Benjamin. And to our parents, Dolly and Bernie Brown and Zelda Steinberg, for their unconditional love and guidance.

Finally, to the late M. K. Steinberg, a special thanks for spending a lifetime teaching his daughter, Barbara, that money can never equal the love between child and parent.

SECTION ONE

• • •

Looking for Success in All the Wrong Places

CHAPTER ONE

A Time of Reckoning

Today a new sun rises for me; everything lives, everything is animated, everything seems to speak to me of my passion, everything invites me to cherish it.
— ANNE DE LENCLOS

Quick! Define what success means to you. A prestigious job title? An impressive salary? A corner office with a view? Power and perks?

Traditionally, these have been the yardsticks used to measure one's success. But as we stand on the threshold of the twenty-first century, the nature and meaning of work are undergoing a profound revolution—particularly for women. Indeed, a burgeoning number of women appear to be finding themselves at an emotional—and even spiritual—crossroads.

Caroline is one such woman. Forty-five years old and an executive vice president at a Fortune 100 company, she appears to have it all: an elegant home, a successful husband, two beautiful children, a live-in nanny, a fancy car, and a fat bank account. Yet, despite these outward trappings of success, Caroline feels hollow inside and dangerously out of balance.

"My entire life is work," she admits. "In my quest for success, I have neglected family and friends, and when I look at who I've become, I don't particularly like what I see. All of my hard work and the tangible rewards it's brought me have not given me the joy and peace of mind I thought they would. Sure, on the outside, I *appear* successful. But I keep wondering, 'Is this all there is?'"

Caroline, we have discovered in our research, is far from alone. Despite their stunning achievements, scores of successful women like her report feeling the same: empty, disillusioned, and unfulfilled.

MAKING HEADLINES

PULITZER PRIZE–WINNING *NEW YORK TIMES* COLUMNIST GIVES UP NEWSPAPER CAREER . . . MICROSOFT'S HIGHEST RANKING WOMAN RESIGNS . . . FIRST FEMALE TO HEAD UP FDIC STEPS DOWN . . . PEPSI PRESIDENT CALLS IT QUITS.

What gives? In the '80s, women bought into the traditional notion of success: the prestigious job title and six-figure income. But now many are discovering that they want much more than the bottom line provides. They resent being married to their jobs. Instead of doing more and more and enjoying it less and less, they seek lives that are more multidimensional. They long for sufficient quality time to devote to family, friends, community, and other outside interests, as well as time for solitude and self-reflection to balance how much of themselves they typically give away. They yearn to feel that who they are and what they do matters. They want the workplace to be more than a place to earn their daily bread. In essence, money is not enough.

"Women are discovering that work isn't enough," confirms Los Angeles organizational psychologist Anna Graham, Ph.D. "They're also realizing that when you make work the center of your universe, you lose diversity in your life and end up not only feeling out of touch with the rest of the world, but out of touch with yourself."

Women who are consumed by the demands of work also risk losing their sense of purpose. "And purpose is not only what you do; it is who you are," Graham adds. "Regardless of your choice of career paths, it is purpose—not salary or recognition—that gives your work meaning. And sooner or later, an absence of meaning is not only frustrating, but robs your life of zest and joy."

Clearly, this is a time of reckoning for working women, and that, in a nutshell, is the focus of this book. For years, far too many women—grateful and even flattered by opportunities to climb the corporate ladder—have taken whatever was offered to them without pausing to consider their own needs. They have followed the advice of mentors rather than listening to their own hearts and playing to their own strengths. So busy trying to prove themselves, many have lost sight of their own values, as well as control of their own lives. And in the process of constantly trying to meet others' expectations, these women have let others define their own destinies.

But no longer.

This book, through a series of thought-provoking and inspirational stories, will show you how growing numbers of women are beginning to redefine success in a variety of ways.

For example, some, whose careers have advanced far

beyond their wildest dreams—but who have also paid a high price for success in terms of personal sacrifice—have decided to put the brakes on and exit the rat race. Others have opted to step off the promotion path—at least temporarily—to regain their footing and sense of equilibrium. Many have elected to move down the ladder a notch or two and replace their exhausting and all-consuming careers with positions offering less pressure, lower visibility, and greater personal satisfaction. And while some of these women have struggled a bit financially as a result, few have any regrets.

Of course, not all women are leaving or changing their jobs. Instead, they are changing *themselves*. No longer willing to postpone happiness, they are taking deliberate steps to sort out and separate what's really important to them in life from all the glitz and glitter.

Many women we spoke with suffered from boredom—not burnout—and have decided to look elsewhere for jobs that offer meaning and purpose, or have turned to community work to fill the void. In their quest for success, staggering numbers of women we interviewed have launched their own businesses. And the most common reason they cited for venturing out on their own? Control—of their time, their futures, and their financial destinies. Surprisingly few, however, seem exclusively motivated by money. In fact, scores of female entrepreneurs we spoke with have found ways to integrate profits *and* meaning.

Naturally, many of today's working women who are redefining success cut their teeth working in corporate America—rising through the ranks, then bumping their heads on a glass ceiling. Sadly, in their futile efforts to reach the top, many worked so hard at trying to "fit in" and meet the expectations of their bosses and colleagues, that somewhere along the way they lost track of themselves. Many of them are now redefining success by recovering their identities.

Finally, perhaps never is there a greater need for women to redefine success than when the work-family equation is thrown off kilter. The good news is that scores of working mothers are devising ways—through job sharing, flextime, telecommuting, and even taking a few years off—to find serenity and sanity.

As writers and consultants, we have devoted ourselves to chronicling the development of women in the workplace. Six years ago, we published our first book together, *More Power to You!* This book showed women how to communicate their way to success. Three years later, we wrote *Swim with the Dolphins,* a book filled with tips and stories showing how female managers could succeed—and were succeeding—on their own terms.

While crisscrossing the country to give lectures, workshops, and seminars for working women, one dominant concern has emerged: the quest for meaning and balance in one's life. As women have become more and more successful in traditional terms, they have come to question the *real* meaning of success. This rampant ambivalence is what led us to focus in this book on what is perhaps the most important work-related issue of our time: winning at work without losing at life.

In our research, we have discovered many women who have taken the steps necessary for them to have successful careers without sacrificing family, fun, and a sense of balance and well-being. The number one lesson they've taught us is that success is a very personal thing. We hope that this book will help you define and create a definition of success that fulfills *your* needs, *your* goals, and *your* dreams.

CHAPTER TWO

The Evolution of Superwoman

If I have to, I can do anything. I am strong; I am invincible. I am woman!

— HELEN REDDY

THE '60S: AGAINST ALL ODDS

The year was 1962, and Maria Rossini had just received her master's degree in architecture from Berkeley University. Having sailed through the program on a full scholarship, she had impeccable credentials and high hopes of landing a plum position in her field. But she also knew that being female might work against her, so she whipped up a résumé using initials in place of her first and middle names. When a prestigious Berkeley firm invited her for an interview, she was elated.

Less than five minutes into her interview, however, Rossini's hopes were dashed when the interviewer began concocting lame excuses regarding why his firm couldn't possibly hire her. "They told me the draft stools were too high for women's dresses, that my presence would be disruptive to the men in the office, and that my accent was a problem," recalls the fifty-seven-year-old Philippines native who now owns her own firm in Atlanta.

Like Rossini, many women coming of age in the '60s boasted college degrees. A vast majority, however, stayed at home to keep house and raise children. Many did this not necessarily by choice, but because they lacked the emotional support of their husbands and families to pursue a career.

Not that jobs weren't available for women during this tumultuous decade. On the contrary, they were plentiful—if you could teach, type, or nurse. But unless you were a woman born into a family that owned and operated a business, managerial and executive positions were virtually nonexistent.

Besides, who wanted to work for lousy pay? Granted, the working climate improved for women once the government stepped in, passing the Equal Pay Act of 1963. Fresh on its heels came the Civil Rights Act of 1964 that banned discrimination against women. Nevertheless, women were still barred from a slew of challenging and well-paying positions simply because they weren't considered "suitable." After all, most of the corporate sector at the time was controlled by white males over fifty, who, as Janet Wylie points out in her book *Chances and Choices: How Women Can Succeed in Today's Knowledge-Based Businesses,* "firmly believed that women belonged in the kitchen, the bedroom, and anyplace but the boardroom."

THE '70S: MAKING HEADWAY

Thankfully, the '70s marked the beginning of a transformation in the lives of women that would change the country—and the workplace—forever. Many women went to graduate and professional schools, and women began pouring into the workforce in unprecedented numbers. In fact, by 1972, a whopping 43 percent of adult American women were working outside the home—earning on average 59.4 cents for every dollar men earned—and for the first time in history, working wives outnumbered housewives.

That same year, *Ms.* magazine made its debut, serving as a true sign of the times. Pictured on its cover was a woman with eight arms juggling a typewriter, a frying pan, an iron, a telephone, a mirror, a steering wheel, a clock, and a rake. The magazine sold out within a week; the women's movement had arrived.

"How well I remember the '70s," says Laura Shipley, who landed her first job as a manager for a national hotel chain in 1973. "I had just gotten my MBA from an Ivy League university and was fiercely proud to be just one of a handful of female faces in my graduating class. The job I took was a stepping-stone to the executive suite—or so I thought." But climbing that ladder—Shipley eventually made it to vice president of finance before she resigned, got married, and started a family—was "tough, exhausting, and incredibly lonely," she adds.

Indeed, women who managed to penetrate the upper echelons of corporate America in the '70s were pioneers. "We had no role models, no mentors, and so many pressures to prove ourselves," Shipley recalls.

Many also paid a high price. "Trying to fit in was virtually impossible," explains Shipley. "Naturally, our consensus-building ways clashed with the command-and-control styles that dominated corporate America at the time. Generally speaking, male colleagues and superiors viewed us as weak, unable to make decisions, incompetent, and manipulative. And yet, those of us who tried to assert ourselves, flaunt our talents, and take control were criticized and shunned. It was a no-win situation!"

Promotions were painstakingly slow to come by as well. For example, Rossini, who took a job with an Atlanta architectural firm in the '70s, recalls, "I worked my way up to associate before hitting a brick wall. The firm I worked for kept passing me over for promotions and raises I deserved. They'd say, 'You do great work, but yours is a second income. Surely you can understand why we have to reward the men in this office first. Even though your work is better than theirs, they have families to support.'" It was that kind of mentality that led to Rossini's defection from the firm in 1983, when she decided she could fare just as well—if not better—on her own.

THE '80S: "SHOW ME THE MONEY"

Fast-forward to the '80s and a brighter picture emerges. Gung-ho on trying to prove themselves, women made significant headway in every occupation imaginable, including those traditionally reserved for men.

Strength in numbers helped to fuel the frenzy. Indeed, women accounted for 62 percent of the workforce growth of the '80s. By decade's end, nearly fifty-seven million women were bringing home paychecks. Just over twenty million of these were mothers—up from sixteen million in 1980. And, for the first time ever, women were reaching senior ranks in significant numbers. By the late '80s, 30 percent of women were managers or executives (compared with 29 percent of men).

More good news: the average woman's income jumped 11 percent (while the typical man's earnings fell 7 percent), and the average salary of top executive women nearly doubled.

But despite this quantum leap, a dark side was surfacing. With life moving at warp speed, many women who had bought into the notion that they could do it all—and be it all—began to grow weary, cranky, and disillusioned: weary of juggling family life and impossible work loads, cranky about still having to prove themselves in a male-dominated workforce, and disillusioned at having to make so many trade-offs and personal sacrifices to succeed.

Few, however, dared to speak up or take action. After all, in so many ways, women had finally arrived. Wasn't this what they wanted and had collectively fought for for so long? Shouldn't they be ecstatic with the amazing progress they'd made and the many opportunities they now had? Indeed, with all the hype and hoopla along the way, to mess with success, to complain, or to give up the fight would somehow smack of betrayal—right?

Lois Crosby thought so. This mother of four spent most of the '80s working for a large real estate corporation on the West Coast, slowly fighting her way up the ladder from senior accountant to senior vice president. "I had it all," she quips. "All the drudge work at the office, and all the responsibilities for domestic chores and child care at home, that is! In fact, my life was a marathon."

But Crosby, like many other women who shared her predicament, rarely complained. "Sure it was a grind, but I had a fairly high-level position and a substantial income of my own," she reports. "And that was important to me." Nevertheless, an impressive title and a hefty paycheck couldn't ultimately sustain her. "Eventually, all the juggling began to take its toll, and I was exhausted. I could never seem to find a minute to relax. I was like that Energizer bunny—always going . . . and going . . . and going."

Crosby's turning point came in 1988, courtesy of Erma Bombeck. "My mother, who had been chiding me for years about working too hard, sent me one of Bombeck's clippings. The topic was Superwomen, and a portion of it read: 'We've been so busy impressing everyone with how we are faster than a speeding bullet, more powerful than a locomotive, and able to leap tall buildings in a single bound, that we've set a standard for future generations that is downright frightening.'"

That passage hit home for Crosby. "Just a week earlier, when I'd taken my six-year-old daughter, Stacy, in for her annual checkup, the pediatrician asked her what she wanted to be when she grew up. Stacy thought for a minute, then said, 'I want to be a father.' And when the puzzled doctor asked why, she explained, 'Because mommies work too hard.'"

In 1989, Crosby was offered a partnership at her firm, but turned it down. Six months later, she left the company altogether to launch a small accounting business from her home. "My business is still going," says Crosby, now fifty-five. "But I've intentionally kept it small so that I could have plenty of time for both my family and myself."

THE '90S: FROM BOOM TO BUST

Just prior to 1990, our nation's economy went belly-up. Sweeping changes occurred as the United States shifted from an industrial- to an information-based society and joined the global economy. By the time the dust settled, virtually every company and organization still afloat had undergone drastic downsizing or radical restructuring, making competition for choice jobs tighter than ever.

The good news: stiff global competition changed the rules of business. With a new emphasis on teamwork, raising productivity, and motivating the workforce, the old command-and-control style of management became obsolete. Finally, women—with their collaborative and consensus-building ways—were a hot commodity.

When the workplace was ready for them, many women decided to opt out. With fewer people left to handle already overwhelming workloads, many preferred instead to do some downsizing and restructuring of their own.

"There has been a definite shift from a career ethic to a self-fulfillment ethic," confirms Dana Friedman, co-president of the Families and Work Institute in New York. "In the '80s, women were willing to make sacrifices to move up the ladder. They still want to contribute and succeed, but they also want to organize their careers in a way that they see fit, not in a way defined by other people."

In 1991, Mary Wagner was earning close to six figures in salary and commission as a sales manager for an insurance company headquartered in the Midwest. "It was a career I'd fallen into after graduating from Indiana University," she says. "I had a master's degree in education, but at the time there were few teaching positions available. I'd always been a crackerjack salesperson and desperately needed an income. The company I went to work for was making a concerted effort to hire more women, and I happened to be in the right place at the right time."

But competition in the insurance business is fierce, and despite her success, Wagner soon regretted her career choice. "The money was great, but work was a real pressure cooker. I could never seem to catch my breath, nor rest on my laurels," she recalls. "Sales figures for my division were consistently among the highest in the company, and they soared every year by 10 to 20 percent. Nevertheless, there were constant and enormous pressures from my boss to continue breaking records. In fact, instead of praising me for a job well done, he'd always demand to know, 'What are your goals for *next* month?' It was a suffocating environment, and after just three years in the business, I felt tired, tense, and frazzled all the time."

In 1994, when Wagner's company was bought out by a larger firm, she saw the writing on the wall. "New owners typically clean house," she explains. And she was right.

But rather than have her name placed in the potential layoff pool, Wagner opted to resign and go back to her first love: teaching. "Now I work eight-hour days nine months a year and leave school every day feeling that what I do is important," she says. "I also feel appreciated by my principal, as well as my students and their parents. Granted, I took a decisive cut in salary and have had to make some major readjustments in my lifestyle. But I'm far more content. I guess I finally realized that the real bottom line is being able to enjoy life."

A RETURN TO FAMILY VALUES

Family values are making a huge comeback in the '90s, which has spurred many working women—torn between careers and kids—to give up the juggling act altogether. Others are finding salvation in modern-day solutions like flextime and working at home.

In 1994, Anna Quindlen had one of the highest-profile jobs in journalism. As the sole female voice on the *New York Times* op-ed page, she had won a Pulitzer Prize in 1992 for her syndicated columns, and many had her pegged as the future managing editor of the country's most prestigious newspaper. But climbing the corporate ladder at the *Times* was not part of Quindlen's personal game plan. In fact, in her home office—perched just above the telegram she received announcing her Pulitzer Prize—is a framed quote that reads: THE KEY TO SUCCESS: FOLLOW YOUR HEART. And after almost twenty-five years in the newspaper business, Quindlen had decided to do just that.

Already leading a double life—in addition to writing for the *Times,* Quindlen had already published two successful novels—she craved more time to write prose and a life that wasn't so public. "My children were also behind my decision—as they have been behind literally every life decision made since my eldest was born," she wrote in an article entitled "Why I Quit" for *Working Woman.* "They have given me the perspective on the pursuit of joy and the passage of time. I miss too much when I am out of their orbit, and as they grow, like a time-lapse photograph that makes a flower out of a bud in scant minutes, I understand that I will have time to pursue a more frantic agenda when they have gone on to pursue their own. But they have made a more frantic agenda seem somehow less seductive."

IN SEARCH OF PERSONAL FULFILLMENT

Like Quindlen, many women are deciding that maybe it's time they caught their balance and sought personal fulfillment for a change. Jacqueline Sa counted her blessings when she was recruited right out of college in 1978 to work for AT&T. Over the next decade, she led a charmed life, professionally speaking, earning a series of promotions that landed her in the executive suite. Happily married to another AT&T executive, she says in retrospect that all that was missing from her life was time.

Indeed, Sa regularly put in twelve-hour days at the office, and because she had responsibility for overseas business clients, was barraged with telephone calls and e-mail messages around the clock. "I was well compensated," she acknowledges, "but I had no personal time to spend any of the money I was making. Soon my health began to suffer, and eventually my marriage fell apart."

In 1988, Sa traded her AT&T job for a management position in Philadelphia. With the grueling hours and heavy travel schedule, however, feelings of déjà vu soon began to haunt her. "There was a lot of international travel involved," she reports. "Sometimes I'd be visiting five countries in two weeks. And while that may *sound* glamorous, it was exhausting."

The day she uncharacteristically snapped at a pregnant manager who told Sa she couldn't work on Saturdays served as a wake-up call. "When I went home, I felt so awful. I had become a corporate machine," she remembers thinking. "I couldn't care less about anyone else's personal life, because I had none of my own." Seven months after starting her new job, Sa announced she was leaving. "The company thought I was angling for more money and tried to sweeten the deal," she says. "But what I wanted—and needed most—wasn't negotiable."

Following several months of soul searching, Sa found her niche. "I had spent the weekend with my boyfriend in Conestoga at a holistic spa that caters to couples and was not impressed," she recalls. "On the drive home, both of us were lost in our own thoughts when Roy broke the silence and said exactly what I was thinking: 'If I had my own spa, it would be so different.' It may sound crazy, but the fact that Roy—who really isn't a spiritual person at all—and I were on the same wavelength, gave me the unmistakable feeling that this was meant to be."

Within nine months, Sa and Roy Nee had built Tea Garden Springs from scratch. "It's a wonderful, pampering place that emphasizes healing and holistic health. Doing this was risky and scary, but in my heart, I knew it would be a success." In fact, Tea Garden Springs has become the talk of the spa world and is used by many in the industry as a model. The business is still young, which means grueling hours at times for Sa. But looking ahead two to three years, she plans to turn the day-to-day operations over to the managers she is currently training and cut back to working only three to four days a week.

"Sure, life is a bit stressful at the moment, as I grow this business," she adds. "But I do my work now with a sense of usefulness that I never felt in corporate America. I feel as if I'm fulfilling a mission. I'm helping people to embrace body, mind, and spirit in all they do, and that's incredibly important and satisfying to me."

NOT JUST A FLEETING PHENOMENON

Yankelovich Partners, a leading market-research firm, recently surveyed three hundred career women, ages thirty-five to forty-nine, about their feelings regarding work and life. By society's definition, these were highly successful women—94 percent were managers or executives, and over half earned salaries of more than $60,000. Yet, all but 13 percent said they had made, or were seriously considering making, a major change in their lives. Almost a third said they frequently felt depressed. More than 40 percent said they felt trapped, and a majority complained that they didn't have a personal life.

Signs are everywhere that the '90s are shaping up—at least for working women—to be the decade of our discontent. Throughout the '60s, '70s, and '80s, it seemed achievement enough just to make it in a man's world. But that small, persistent voice could not be stifled—the one that kept whispering, "There must be more to life."

In essence, somewhere along the way, it appears that far too many of us lost our balance. Money became too enticing, or we let work become our anchor. In short, in our quest for success, we have allowed our careers to control us. And now is the time to do something about it.

CHAPTER THREE

When Having It All Isn't Enough

So often I have listened to everyone else's truth and tried to make it mine. Now, I am listening deep inside for my own voice and I am softly, yet firmly, speaking my own truth.
—LIANE CORDES

In a recent column to the readers of *Working Woman* magazine, editor-in-chief Lynn Povich wrote, "It seems that almost every conversation I have these days revolves around carving out more time or money—or both—to live the way we want. Obviously, it took a certain amount of success to get to this point; we needed to accomplish something in the world before we could sit back and ask whether we had gotten what we truly wanted. It may be a luxury that no other generation of working women has ever had. Yet our hard-earned success is not paying off in some fundamental ways."

The classic American definition of success has typically revolved around money and all the material things it can buy. But, as Harvard economist and author of *The Overworked American* Juliet Schor notes, "Affluence is not delivering the kind of meaning and satisfaction it promised." Consequently, women's (and many men's) definitions of success are flip-flopping.

When *Working Woman* recently commissioned the Roper Organization to ask 1,027 Americans how they measured success, 53 percent of both women and men said their definition of "being successful" had changed in the last five years. Two-thirds agreed that "making money isn't as important to me." In fact, a whopping 86 percent agreed (59 percent strongly) that they would "rather make an adequate salary doing a job that makes the world a better place than just earn a lot of money." And what makes these findings particularly significant is that women in every age and racial group tended to share this sentiment.

"We're seeing the demise of conspicuous consumption," agrees Barbara Caplan, a director of Yankelovich Partners. "A few years ago, when we asked people what they thought symbolized success, most respondents chose material things like expensive furs, shopping at fancy stores, and having a million dollars. That hasn't disappeared, but people now say they're more interested in being in control of their lives and feeling satisfied with life."

Similar feelings surfaced in a comprehensive quality-of-life poll conducted by *U.S. News & World Report* and the advertising agency Bozell Worldwide, Inc. Just over half (51 percent) of those surveyed said they would rather have more time for themselves—even if it meant making less money. Half also said that in the past five years, they had taken steps to simplify their lives—like moving to a community that offered a less hectic lifestyle, lowering their commitments or expectations, and declining promotions. "People say they are pretty satisfied with their jobs but are searching for new simplicity," says *U.S. News* pollster Ed Goeas, who, with Celinda Lake, consulted on the survey. "They are uneasy about the time they are spending on the job, and some are already trying to act on it. For others, it's a looming conflict."

A 1995 poll commissioned by the Merck Family Fund revealed that many Americans are willingly trading in prosperity in the form of paychecks for the kind of peace of mind having more free time offers. When asked, "In the last five years, have you voluntarily made changes in your life which resulted in your making less money?" 28 percent of the poll's respondents said yes.

Demographers call this trend "downshifting"—and women appear to be leading the way. In the Merck poll, for example, 32 percent of the female respondents reported voluntarily downshifting, compared with 23.5 percent of male respondents. And among working mothers who were surveyed, 45 percent reported cutting back on earnings, and 87 percent said they wanted to spend more time caring for their kids. But it's not just women who yearn to get out of the fast lane. In a recent Gallup Poll, one-third of American couples said they were ready to take a 20 percent pay cut if it meant they or their spouses could work fewer hours.

Evidence that priorities are shifting—and that money is no longer enough—emerged from the *Working Woman*/Roper Poll as well. Almost half of those surveyed said that their lives were becoming much more centered on relationships, self-fulfillment, and spiritual values. Specifically, there was far less emphasis on "money and material things" and far more on "people and satisfaction," as well as "personal growth and contentment."

Good Housekeeping also teamed up with Roper to ask women to define the American Dream. The results: Getting rich ranked dead last on their fourteen-point list. At the top: "A happy family life" (77 percent), "having enough time for family and friends" (65 percent), and "being in control of one's life" (57 percent).

Finally, when *Working Woman* recently gathered three dozen top executive women from across the country to talk about success, a surprising number said they now view it as "a means rather than an end, a power tool that can be used to widen doors and knock out walls in a society badly in need of remodeling."

NOT JUST A MOM'S PROBLEM

Perhaps most surprising about all this research is that motherhood appears to have little correlation with the feelings of disillusionment and frustration so many women are reporting. For example, in a recent Yankelovich Poll of three hundred career women ages thirty-five to forty-nine, 87 percent said they'd made, or were seriously considering making, a major change in their lives. Almost a third reported feeling frequently depressed. Over 40 percent said they felt trapped, and a majority complained of having no personal life. Notably, women without children felt equally discontented!

Another case in point: in the early '90s, Deloitte & Touche, a Fortune 500 firm, set out to pinpoint the reasons behind an unusually high turnover rate among its up-and-coming female employees. As is true in many companies, executives assumed that women were bailing out primarily for family reasons. What they found after talking to eighty women who had left the firm, however, was that only a handful (less than 12 percent) were staying at home to care for small children—and most of them planned to go back to work. The rest were working elsewhere—two-thirds had full-time jobs, and 20 percent were working flextime.

"That blew apart the theory that women were leaving to take care of their kids," says Ellen Gabriel, a partner at Deloitte & Touche. In response, the firm has since launched an ambitious gender-awareness training program for its five thousand partners and managers, which is designed to retain and promote more women.

Surprisingly, the glass ceiling doesn't seem to have much bearing on women's current levels of frustration, either. Despite that half of those surveyed by Yankelovich felt their workplaces were overly dominated by men, more than 70 percent expected to make major career advances in the next five years.

THE BIG GULP?

So what *are* the reasons behind women's growing discontent? "There is some kind of profound something going on—a reassessment, a rethinking, a big gulp, whatever," confirms Ann Clurman, a partner at Yankelovich. "I think it has to do with self-image and the workplace."

But Harold Kushner, author of numerous best-sellers, including *When All You've Ever Wanted Isn't Enough*, attributes these changing attitudes and seemingly sudden needs to redefine success to a much deeper problem. "It is our souls that need caring for," he says. "And our souls are not hungry for fame, comfort, wealth or power. These rewards create almost as many problems as they solve. Our souls are hungry for meaning, for the sense that we have figured out how to live so that our lives matter, so that the world will be at least a little bit different for our having passed through it."

MORE THAN A MIDLIFE CRISIS

Some experts have used the term "midlife crisis" to explain working women's new search for balance, meaning, and purpose. But numerous studies reveal that this phenomenon is in no way limited to baby boomers. For example, UCLA's Higher Education Research Institute has found for five years running that the percentage of college freshmen in the United States who consider it important to be "very well off financially" has dropped, while the percentage interested in "developing a meaningful philosophy of life" has risen.

"Corporate recruiters are seeing a surprising trend this season on undergraduate campuses," adds *Wall Street Journal* columnist Sue Shellenbarger. "Questions about work-balance—which in the past were saved for the final round of interviews, or never asked at all—are surfacing in job candidates' first-round talks with employers." Moreover, questions ranging from "Do people who work for you have a life off the job?" and "Do your employees get to see much of their families?" to "What support can you offer my spouse?" and "Do you offer flextime?" are coming from both married and single recruits.

Indeed, the forty-six million Generation Xers, or baby busters—now between the ages of twenty and thirty-three—are radically different from their predecessors. How? "For starters, they expect work-life balance from day one," says Maury Hanigan of Hanigan Consulting Group, New York, strategic staffing specialists. And while Generation Xers have often been accused of being selfish and self-centered, keep in mind that many of these were kids of working parents who didn't see that much of their moms and dads growing up and are determined to avoid the same pattern. "These were the latchkey kids," confirms Hanigan. "They had stressed-out parents who saw them for twenty minutes before they went to bed. Then their parents were laid off, and they said, 'This equation doesn't make sense to me.'"

Historically speaking, most generations have looked to their predecessors as role models and mentors. Not Generation Xers. According to Faith Wohl, former head of DuPont's Work-Family Initiatives Program, who's now director of the Office of Workplace Initiatives and the U.S. General Services Administration, "Today's twenty-something women are looking at the failed Superwoman, and they're revolting against the mindless careerism they saw their sisters or mother have."

To jump-start their careers, many baby boomers postponed having children until their mid-thirties or later. The trend among Generation Xers, however, is to have kids first, then maybe work part-time for a few years before pursuing a serious career. In other words, children—not work—are top priority, and if that means sacrificing perks and promotions, so be it.

Besides, a burning desire to climb to the top of the career ladder doesn't appear to be a top priority for most Generation Xers. In fact, in a recent Roper Poll of eighteen- to twenty-nine-year-olds, a mere 26 percent said they aspired to the boss's job—down from 41 percent eight years earlier.

Yet, despite these glaring differences between baby boomers and busters, there is common ground. A recent study by the Families and Work Institute found that—just like the growing numbers of today's successful working women in their forties and fifties—both men *and* women in their twenties view family life—not careers—as the single most important route to self-fulfillment. Money is nice, they say, but working excessive hours is out of the question.

"Xers don't have the all-consuming I-am-defined-by-my-work ethos," says Karen Ritchie, who studied Generation X as director of Media Services for the Detroit office of the advertising agency McCann Erickson. "They're ambitious, but their ambition is to be well-rounded."

STRENGTH IN NUMBERS

All of this, of course, bodes well for the coming millennium. For as competition for the best and brightest workers heats up—and with boomers and busters in agreement that your life is your career, and not vice versa—corporate America simply can't afford not to listen.

SECTION TWO

• • •

*Rewards Beyond the Bottom Line:
Tales of Women Who Are Redefining
Success on Their Own Terms*

CHAPTER FOUR

All Work and No Play: Exiting the Rat Race

The trouble with the rat race is that even if you win, you're still a rat.

—LILY TOMLIN

In October of 1997, when Brenda Barnes, president and chief executive of Pepsi Cola North America, decided to call it quits, a media frenzy followed. Her story made front page news in the *Wall Street Journal* and *USA Today*. Articles and interviews in *Harper's, U.S. News & World Report,* and on *The Today Show* quickly followed.

Barnes is not the only woman in recent years to make headlines because of her decision to resign from a high-profile position. And what's the driving force behind these bailouts? A personal choice to shift priorities and a firm belief that self-fulfillment is far more critical to success than power, prestige, and personal profit.

A JOB THAT LOST ITS FIZZ

Barnes, forty-three, was one of corporate America's highest-ranking women when she announced that she was stepping down. She had spent half her life at PepsiCo, but after years of hectic travel, dinner meetings, missing children's birthdays, and even living in separate cities from her husband as they both pursued their careers, Barnes felt she had lost her balance. "I have made a lot of trade-offs for Pepsi, and now I need to give my family more of my time," she said.

Quick not to point the finger at Pepsi's management for the demands of her time, however, Barnes stated, "If you want to be president and CEO, that's a choice you have to make. I don't expect any slack to be cut." She also credited her husband and boss for their support over the years. "I don't think I could have got to where I am if I didn't have Randy as such a supportive spouse and Craig as a boss."

But, she added, "You have to make choices—and maybe I burned the candle at both ends for too long."

SAVING HER SOUL

In late 1996, Patty Stonesifer stunned colleagues at Microsoft Corporation by announcing her intention to resign. The highest-ranking woman at the world's largest software company, Stonesifer had risen through the ranks to head up Microsoft's Interactive Media Division. During her eight-year tenure, Stonesifer used her magical touch to transform several of the company's troubled divisions into success stories. She was also instrumental in forming the much ballyhooed joint venture between Microsoft and Dreamworks SKG, a $30 million project designed to fill cyberspace with movie-quality games and adventures.

But despite the fact that she enjoyed her work, this forty-one-year-old mother of two teenagers decided she needed to escape the pressure-cooker work environment at Microsoft and spend more time with her family. "I had a lot of flexibility on the job, but I realized I'd been giving my soul to Microsoft and needed to slow down," she says. "I still wanted to work—but at a different scale."

Striking out on her own as a consultant, Stonesifer's first client was Dreamworks. And her second was Bill Gates, who persuaded her to head up the Gates Library Foundation. Started with an unprecedented cash donation of $200 million from Microsoft's CEO—and supplemented by $200 million in Microsoft software—the Foundation's mission is to provide computers and Internet access to libraries in low-income areas. "We'll be working with more than half of the seventeen thousand libraries in North America," reports Stonesifer, who is ecstatic about landing a job she can sink "both my heart and head into."

Although it's an ambitious project she has taken on, Stonesifer insists she has not jumped from the frying pan to the fire. "I'm only working three days a week," she reports, "and I'm taking plenty of vacation days." Indeed, over the summer, she took her sixteen-year-old to Africa and has winter plans to take her thirteen-year-old to Italy.

IN SEARCH OF NEW HORIZONS

In March of 1997, just past the halfway point of her five-year term, Ricki R. Helfer, chair of the Federal Deposit Insurance Corporation (FDIC), announced her resignation. The first woman to head a federal bank regulatory agency, Helfer had accepted the post three years earlier at the tail end of a turbulent decade for the banking industry. Major challenges she faced included cutting—by a third—a staff that had swollen to 12,115 to handle the more than sixteen hundred bank and thrift failures that occurred during the late '80s and early '90s.

Colleagues were surprised by Helfer's early departure. After all, during her short stay, commercial bank earnings rose 7.5 percent to a record high of $52.4 million, while savings institutions registered profits of $7 billion. But Helfer, fifty-two, said in a letter to President Clinton that she wanted to "spend more time with my husband and family and consider new opportunities and challenges."

HOW COULD THEY?

When Anna Quindlen stepped down from her position at the *New York Times,* the publishing world's reaction was one of shock and suspicion. "Some of the people who wanted to know why I left asked my friends, 'Did Anna find out she was being passed over for the top editor's job?' It couldn't be that I said, 'The *New York Times* is a great institution, but some things about it don't meet my needs anymore,'" she says. "It had to be, 'She couldn't cut the mustard' or 'At base, she's really a girl.' In order to make sense of it, they had to estrogenize it.

It couldn't be that there was a greater source of satisfaction based on your own assessment of what you want. Instead it was, 'She wanted to spend more time on the playground,' which completely ignores the fact that I've spent so much of my time on the playground over the last twelve years that I can seesaw and think about welfare reform at the same time without breaking a sweat."

Indeed, instead of applauding her gutsy move, even women felt betrayed by Quindlen's decision. "How could she let our side down?" many wondered about this accomplished journalist seen as having it all. But Quindlen made no apologies and insisted she was never the Superwoman some perceived her to be. "No one's having it all," she told *People* magazine before her resignation. "I'm pretty happy, but I spend every day thinking about what's fallen through the cracks. Was I short-tempered with the kids? Did I give a fine enough polish to my column because I had to pick up somebody at a play date? You're always robbing Peter to pay Paul."

Still others questioned, "How could you give up the power?" But Quindlen believes that "power is the power to do what you want. That's my whole impulse in life, to be able to do what I want."

Barnes's departure from Pepsi sparked a similar nationwide debate. Some criticized her move—or at least her frankness about why she was exiting the rat race. "This has set the rest of us back a long time," complained one female caller to the *Wall Street Journal* after the story broke. "It verifies all the worst stereotypes about women in the workplace." Others, however, found her honesty refreshing. Another caller—this one male—appeared delighted with Barnes's actions. "She proved that you can't have it all, be supermom and superexecutive, too. Men can't have it all either."

Some fretted that Barnes's resignation had even caused such a stir. One caller, a broadcast consultant, asked, "What state is our society in, that deciding to take care of your kids is headline news?" Still others predicted that Barnes's retirement would be short-lived. And, in fact, she herself didn't rule out taking another corporate job down the road. "I can't say what I'll be doing for the rest of my life," she remarked. "I'm not checking out on life."

Wall Street Journal columnist Sue Shellenbarger agreed. "I wouldn't be surprised if after she regains her balance with her family, Brenda Barnes returns to the workplace," she wrote in her "Work and Family" column. "She may find some potent but more balanced leadership role, perhaps overseeing some of those Gen-Xers who take work-life choices in stride. Then, she would help forge a new executive model—one that doesn't require people to sacrifice their lives on the altar of power."

WOMEN IN THE TRENCHES FOLLOWING SUIT

Because of their limelight positions, Quindlen, Stonesifer, Helfer, and Barnes made headlines when they opted to exit the rat race. No one keeps statistics on such matters, but there are thousands more women following suit. You may not read about them on the front pages of newspapers or in magazine cover stories, but their tales are similar and their motives the same.

FINDING TIME TO CLIMB MOUNTAINS

"In 1989, my husband, Bobby, and I were living the high life in Danville, California, a suburb of Berkeley," says Roxanna Niswander, now forty-three. "I was a marketing manager for a computer company, and Bobby was a systems manager for Levi Strauss. Together we were making $100,000 a year, but spending it just as quickly on the basics of a city life—dinners out, work clothes, and a big expensive house."

In January of 1990, all that changed when the couple had their first child. "Suddenly our priorities shifted," Roxanna recalls. "We wanted to devote the bulk of our time and energy to parenting, but we still had to put in sixty-hour work weeks." For years, the couple had dreamed of retiring someday in Aspen, Colorado. Bobby had lived in the area after college, and the two had often vacationed there. "We decided to think about making it our next, rather than our last, stop," Roxanna reports.

During their next visit to the Rockies, the couple's mission was to check out different scenic villages and compile sample budgets to see if a permanent move would be financially feasible. "Steamboat Springs had the lowest cost of living, but there were only three local companies where we might get jobs, and none of them appealed to us," Roxanna says. "So, instead, we began toying with the idea of buying a business with the money we would save by trading our $400,000 house in California for a smaller one in Steamboat Springs."

The couple found a children's clothing store, Steamboat Kids, up for sale and made an offer. In June of 1992, they packed up their belongings and headed east. "Today, Bobby and I are living a better life than we'd ever imagined," Roxanna says. "Now that we're business partners, my husband and I are a team—and our son, Cameron, who's now seven, is our star player. After Cam gets out of school, he joins us at the store until we all go home together."

Roxanna says she and her husband often work twice as hard as they did in corporate America. "But somehow, being surrounded by all this beautiful scenery and doing something we love doing, it doesn't feel stressful at all," she insists. "Of course, there have been sacrifices. We figured we'd need $50,000 a year to get by, and that's about what we're making. We don't eat out as much anymore, but we do have time to climb mountains."

LISTENING TO HER BODY

In 1975, when Christie Richter dropped out of Pennsylvania State University to pursue a secretarial degree at Katherine Gibbs, she never expected she'd end up a successful Wall Street wheeler and dealer five years later. "I felt lost at Penn State and figured I'd learn more marketable skills at Katherine Gibbs," she says.

Indeed, upon graduation, Richter immediately landed a job answering the telephone at a small investment firm. She was so good at helping clients that within a year and a half, she'd worked her way into a sales position at Drexel peddling money market accounts. A lucrative sixteen-year career on Wall Street followed, during which she often earned bonuses that exceeded her salary. But Richter wasn't happy. "I loved my clients, the markets, and the money," she reports. "But I was always having stress disorders, including TMJ and back problems. And my body was telling me to do something different."

Ultimately, Richter decided to take a leave of absence from work, during which she spent most of her time biking long distances, studying yoga, and mastering the massage techniques that had helped her cope for so many years. When she returned to work three months later, it was only to resign. "The second I stepped on the escalator at the World Trade Center, the hair on the back of my neck literally stood up," she recalls. "So I decided it was time to fire myself."

Today, Richter owns Body Wisdom, a yoga and body works studio in Montclair, New Jersey, where she teaches yoga and gives massages to others suffering from the same stresses she once endured. "It's taken a few years, but I'm beginning to make a good living at this," she says, "and I feel so fortunate to be doing what I'm doing. My work is a gift to me, and I finally have a personal life again. There's such joy in all of this."

FROM MANHATTAN MAYHEM TO PORTLAND PEACE

In 1995, Priscilla Grant bid adieu to her power job as managing editor of *Glamour* magazine and moved from the big city to Portland, Maine. "When I announced my decision to fellow New Yorkers, I got an amusing and somewhat unsettling reaction," she writes in an article entitled "Chucking It All" for *New Woman* magazine. "Many knew the wild beauty and small-town charm of the sea coast and could easily imagine themselves plunked down in some picturesque fishing village—for two or three weeks. But invariably, after saying, 'Maine!

Oh, how wonderful!' they would look at me quizzically, with slightly worried frowns, and ask, 'But what will you *do* there?'" The truth is, after thirty years in the magazine business—including stints as executive editor of *Esquire* and managing editor of both *Vogue* and *House and Garden,* Grant yearned for a quieter life and time to write.

The process that led her to Maine had actually begun on a sweltering afternoon in August of 1992. "While stuck in Madison Avenue gridlock, editing an article in the back of a taxi and late for an already twice-canceled gynecologist appointment, I heard my inner voice declare, 'I don't want to be here anymore. I don't want any of this—the traffic, the fumes, the always being rushed, the overwhelming sense of having stayed too long . . . I can't breathe. I need open space, more time, fewer pressures,'" she recalls.

Four years later, the timing was perfect to make her move, Grant decided. With her daughters out of college and living on their own, her nest was empty. The man in her life—equally burned out after serving twenty years as an executive chef for a large restaurant company— seemed open to making a change. She had assets from which to build a nest egg, plus she already owned a lakeside camp in Maine. Nevertheless, Grant worried about being able to churn out enough writing to make an adequate living. She also fretted about losing all her New York connections. "All I knew for sure was that I had to simplify my life, spend more time by myself, and get closer to nature—or I would go slowly crazy," she says.

Less than a year after the move, Grant began feeling settled and content. "Now I actually have to concentrate to recall the Manhattan soundscape I lived in for so many years—the constant noise of traffic, insistent sirens, truck horns, car alarms, shouts, and whistles," she reveals. "If I close my eyes, I can get back the pungent odor of diesel fuel and Chinese food that permeates my old West Side neighborhood. But it seems a lifetime ago that I breathed that air, moved among those crowds, rode the subways, and rushed to the pace of my executive calendar marked with meetings, deadlines, business lunches, staff reviews, dinners, and so forth. Now, tucked away in my sunlit office, hearing only the hiss of the radiator and the hum of my computer, I wonder that it took me so long to get to this place where I own my life instead of snatching bits and pieces of it on the fly."

REDISCOVERING HER ROOTS

On a picture-perfect day in 1987, Tisa Gabriel was sitting in the Plaza in the middle of Santa Fe feeling very frazzled. As director of the New Mexico Arts Division, she had spent eleven years putting in twelve-plus-hour days to finish demanding projects. "I decided then and there that there were more important things than a career— like time for self, time to learn new things, and time for friendships," she recalls. "It was a matter of balance. We work to live; we don't live to work."

The trouble was, Gabriel was thirty-six, single, and had almost no nest egg to fall back on. Nevertheless, she decided to quit her job. "It was a drastic move," she acknowledges. "I didn't have another position lined up. But I wasn't worried. I felt sure I was marketable and that I wouldn't starve to death." Indeed, within three weeks, Gabriel had a job offer from the administrative services of New Mexico's Office of Cultural Affairs. But she accepted it on one condition: that she not have to report to work for three months.

Gabriel spent her sabbatical hiking, fishing, and enjoying the outdoors—often alone, and sometimes with close pals. She also traveled to her native Central America, where she learned to scuba dive and taught English as a second language. "It felt good to rediscover my roots," she says. "I spoke Spanish before I spoke English, but I had buried all that."

Taking time off also enabled Gabriel to start her new job feeling relaxed, refreshed, and determined to keep things that way. "I was not going to spend more than eight hours a day at the office unless it was a four-alarm emergency," she vowed. "I also wanted my job to reflect who I was on the inside." Despite these self-imposed limitations, Gabriel was promoted several times over the new few years. "I started out as a budget analyst, then became a legislative liaison. Now I'm a liaison officer for international programs, which allows me to use my revived Spanish," she says.

In the early '90s, Gabriel took a six-month leave of absence and traveled to Belize again. "This time when I returned to the States, I was the proud half-owner of a live-aboard scuba diving boat," she reports. "Now I go down once a year to check on the business, spend time with my partner, and enjoy the diving."

These days, when Gabriel sits in Sante Fe's Plaza, she is content. "I've got a job I love. I have deeper friendships. I have a business, and I have my Latin connection," she says. "In short, I've got a whole life again."

COOKING UP SERENITY

Cathy Luce has always loved to cook, but she never dreamed she'd be doing it for a living. Yet, in January of 1997, Luce, thirty-four and single, dropped out of corporate America, took a $70,000 pay cut, and launched Magical Meals, a personal chef service. No one, Luce says, was more surprised than she was. "I thought I would always work for a big company, where someone else would take care of all the headaches," she remarks.

Formerly a telecommunications consultant based in Atlanta, Georgia, Luce found her traveling schedule grueling. "I was out of town more than I was home—including weekends—and it was not fulfilling. I lost contact with friends and realized, 'I know that God did not put me on earth to do this kind of work,'" she reports. Turning to a professional career consultant for advice, Luce discovered that cooking was her greatest joy. "Trouble is, I had never thought of it as being a valid business career," she says.

Initially, Luce toyed with the idea of buying a restaurant with her brother or going to cooking school and becoming a chef. Then, one night while surfing the Internet, she found the U.S. Personal Chef Association's home page. "I called them the next day and knew without a doubt that that was what I wanted to do."

Before launching Magical Meals, Luce took a short course from the U.S. Small Business Administration on how to start a business. She then invested about $2,000 to start her venture and began advertising by word-of-mouth.

In no time, Luce had contracts with nearly a full roster of clients. Typically, she visits each one every two weeks, providing menus customized to their tastes: vegetarian, special diets for people with health problems, food for rushed families with kids, etc.

The night before visiting each client, Luce reviews her recipes and cooking setup. The next day she loads up her little red Alfa Romeo with pots, pans, and utensils, shops for food, and heads to the client's home. There she spends most of the day whipping up twenty entrees, leaving food in labeled containers in the refrigerator and freezer, and taking the dirty pots and pans home with her.

By fall of 1997, when her story was featured on CNN, Luce ended up with more business than she could handle. "Right now I'm experiencing how to grow a business," she says. "And for the moment, I've made the decision not to hire more chefs. I don't want to grow too big too fast."

Indeed, Luce has had calls from would-be clients in far-flung suburbs of Atlanta, a lengthy commute from where she lives. But thus far, she's turned them down. " 'You *must* work for me,' " many have insisted." But Luce keeps reminding herself that she *doesn't* have to. "It's scary saying no and making these tough choices, but the last thing I feel like doing is taking on clients that would mean sitting in traffic forty-five minutes each way."

Luce has a real passion for what she's doing and wants to keep it that way. She especially loves being able to stay put in Atlanta. "I try to work just four days a week, reserving Fridays for appointments with my lawyer and accountant as well as volunteer work," she says. Recently, Luce joined an organization that cooks meals for local AIDS patients. "So, most Fridays I still cook—only not for pay." Saturdays and Sundays are her own as well, and Luce adds that she's in heaven being able to take it easy on weekends for a change.

"The worst thing about all this is not knowing all the answers that an entrepreneur needs to know. You can have a lawyer and an accountant and still not be sure you're doing everything right," she says. "The best part is the satisfaction that you feel, being tired at the end of the day, but having this incredible sense that you are doing what you were meant to do."

SALUTING SUCCESS IN HER OWN WAY

When Kathleen Mercker joined the Air Force in 1969, women composed less than 2 percent of the entire armed forces. "My friends and family were astonished and even a bit concerned with my decision," she says. But having put herself through college in just over three years and having bounced around the Northeast working at various jobs, Mercker was looking for adventure and wanted to see the world.

Officer training was exhausting. "We never got enough sleep, and everything was very structured," she reports. "But the academic classes were challenging." Mercker's psyche was tested as well. "The presence of women in the Air Force at that time was not a welcome sight, and a majority of the few women there attempted to fit in by acting like men," says the former college beauty queen. "There was no nurturing whatsoever, but when I graduated (along with twenty-seven other women in a class that started with forty-two women), I felt that I'd achieved something."

Mercker's first assignment was at an Air Force base near San Francisco, where she worked in personnel. "I had serious doubts about my decision then," she recalls.

"As a woman, I wasn't taken seriously, and being so far away from home, I felt incredibly lonely."

A promotion soon made life bearable. Mercker was assigned to work in transportation. "I was in charge of the protocol lounge at the base's passenger terminal, which meant I had to meet and greet VIPs, make lodging arrangements for them, plan their agendas, transport them within the base, and meet any of their special needs. It was a job with high visibility, and I loved it."

In 1973, however, Mercker was assigned to the Philippines. "I wanted to do the same job at Clark Air Force Base there, but I was turned down," she reports. Instead, she was put in charge of the passenger terminal. Her first big assignment was "Operation Homecoming," a program designed to greet, transport, and secure American P.O.W.s arriving in the Philippines after the Vietnam War had ended. "I'll never forget when the first P.O.W. got off the plane," she says. "His first words were, 'God bless America,' and I knew then I was where I belonged."

Yet, despite her successes over the years—she would later be responsible for an entire base airport in Japan and become the first woman in the field of transportation to snag an assignment at the Pentagon—Mercker grew weary of suppressing her personality. "I was known as 'The Ice Lady,'" she says, "and that really bothered me. I had to work so hard to prove my competence. Yet, no matter what I did, the male officers either ignored me or felt threatened by me—and their wives never, ever accepted me. It was a very lonely existence."

By the time she was transferred to Germany during the Gulf War, Mercker was promoted to colonel. "Suddenly, I could meet all the rest of those crusty old colonels eye to eye and b.s. with them," she says. "Finally,

I could show my true personality." But by then, Mercker had had enough. Her job responsibilities in Germany were enormous. "I coordinated the transportation of troops and all vehicles—planes, boats, barges, trains, and trucks—that deployed from Europe to the Gulf, as well as all forms of transportation from the United States to the Gulf that went through Europe," she says. "It was a twenty-four-hour-a-day job, and I was exhausted."

Thus, after two years in Germany, Mercker volunteered to come back to the United States and serve on the faculty at Air War College in Montgomery, Alabama. There, she taught courses in defense economics and strategic management. "In my spare time, I committed to a program off base that ultimately gave me the courage to turn my life around," she says. "It was with a coach affiliated with the Success Unlimited Network—a program that helps people to produce the results and well-being they want—and was my first introduction to how to succeed by leading a balanced and fulfilling life." Meanwhile, the Air Force wanted to send Mercker back to Germany. "There was an even higher position waiting for me with the potential of an eventual promotion to general," she says. "But I had since redefined what success meant to me, and after twenty-six years, retired from the service."

In 1995, Mercker became affiliated with the Success Unlimited Network herself and now operates her own coaching business based out of Atlanta. Initially, she worked mostly with individuals, but she has since moved into the corporate world and hasn't ruled out the idea of someday pitching her services to the armed forces. "I'm passionate about helping others get in touch with what they want out of life," she says. "I only wish I'd had this opportunity years ago."

REASSESSING THE BIG PICTURE

Harvard University researcher Juliet Schor, author of *The Overworked American,* estimates that the typical American employee works an additional 163 hours annually compared to twenty years ago. And perhaps working moms suffer most—logging seventy-six to eighty-nine hours each week in an attempt to juggle the demands of employment, child care, and housework, according to Schor's calculations.

Rampant downsizing, of course, has made matters worse for many American workers. "Companies haven't replaced the employees they eliminated when they downsized," says Carl Palash, chief economist for MCM Money Watch, a financial advisory service. "The remaining workforce has taken up the slack, and that can be painful."

Growing numbers of workers are also complaining that their jobs are increasingly invading time once reserved for relaxation. On average, office workers take just thirty-six minutes for lunch, according to one recent study. And a whopping 73 percent of Americans employed by companies with one hundred or more staffers bring work home on weekends. Twenty-three percent also put in time even while on vacation.

In many respects, technology has helped to ease the burden. But not always. "It hasn't been the liberator we once thought it would be," notes Paula Rayman, an economist and director of The Radcliffe Public Policy Institute. Not only are workers forced to constantly learn and master new computer systems and software, but e-mail, fax machines, and mobile phones can actually *accelerate* the pace of work both by blurring the boundaries between work time and leisure, and by making workers far more accessible once they physically leave the office. Thus, it's little wonder that for so many of us our lives feel lopsided!

The good news is, exiting the rat race has never been more in vogue. Quitting an important and powerful job, for example, is no longer unthinkable—nor, as illustrated earlier in this chapter—all that unusual. Neither is switching jobs—even if it means working for lower but livable wages—or finding a new career even at midlife or beyond.

Indeed, the once prevailing mind-set that to succeed, our careers must take priority over the rest of our lives is quickly—and thankfully—fading. Balance is today's buzzword. Just ask anyone who's exited the rat race, and they'll wholeheartedly agree. For it is balance, not power—and certainly not money—that enables us to enjoy our work, and keeps our lives from spinning out of control. Once you've had a taste of it, you won't ever want to go back.

CHAPTER FIVE

Plateauing on Purpose

Life isn't a matter of milestones, but of moments.
—ROSE KENNEDY

J ust Say No" is a catchphrase taught to American youngsters as part of a sweeping effort to prevent drug abuse in the United States. But for increasing numbers of working women, the phrase is also being used to prevent the physical and psychological abuse that can result from saying "yes" to all-consuming careers.

For a variety of reasons, there are times in many women's careers when it makes sense to refuse promotions, transfers, and jobs that require long hours, frequent travel, or impossible workloads. And whether deciding to pare down, cut back, stay put, or step off the promotion path, plateauing provides women with ways to keep working—but without sacrificing a sense of balance and well-being.

For many, the decision to plateau is personal. Maybe

there are young children at home whose working moms crave more time and energy to enjoy their youngsters as they grow and develop. Or, perhaps there are ailing parents, whose special needs require having a job with plenty of flexibility. For some, choosing to plateau is a matter of having witnessed, firsthand, total burnout among higher-ups and deciding, "Who needs the aggravation?" For others, it's a result of having "been there, done that—and had enough." For others still, the decision to stay put can boil down to something as simple as loving the jobs they already have. But for most, plateauing on purpose is spurred both by a need to achieve balance in their lives and a quest to redefine success on their own terms.

DOING THE RIGHT THING

Denise Larson once made big bucks on Madison Avenue. A vice president at Young & Rubicam, she was wooed away by J. Walter Thompson when that firm offered to double her salary. From there, she moved to Grey Advertising, landing an even more prestigious job with even greater financial rewards. Over the years, her clients included corporate giants like Kodak, Hallmark, and Metropolitan Life. But when her schedule began requiring her to spend four days a week away from her two-year-old daughter, she decided to give it all up. "It wasn't the job," she says. "It was me. I thought, 'I'm thirty-seven, and I don't want to be doing this when I'm forty-seven.'"

Besides, she didn't especially envy her role models. "I saw women above me whose lives I didn't want to lead— every other day at the shrink," she says. "Not that there's anything wrong with shrinks, but it wasn't the way I wanted to be spending my hard-earned money."

In 1993, Larson joined CPC International, a former client, as a market research manager and immediately made it clear that she had no interest in advancing. "That way, I was free to drop off my two daughters at school every morning, plus focus on the kind of work I loved best—talking to customers and creating strategies for various brands."

In 1997, she was approached by The Lord Group, a subsidiary of Young & Rubicam, and asked to become their director of strategic planning. "It was a tempting offer, because it was a job closer to home and back in advertising, which I missed," she says. "But I was very wary of being sucked right back into the grind. Since it was a small agency, however, I decided to chance it."

Larson's fears were unfounded. In fact, at her new job she has even more flexibility. "Here, I work just four days a week and have even more time to spend with my daughters, now five and nine. I also have a staff of two, who are young, energetic, and just as intent as I am to work as close to a nine-to-five day as possible. Still, I've let everyone know, in no uncertain terms, that I am not interested in climbing the ladder at this agency." For Larson, plateauing has meant taking a pay cut of about 20 percent. "It's been somewhat of a strain," she admits, "but it was definitely the right thing to do as a family."

DOING HER OWN THING

Beth Makens Long was the top salesperson at the Illinois mechanical contracting firm where she worked when she got pregnant with her first child. She maintained her usual hectic schedule—practically up to the minute her son was born—and even negotiated a $275,000 sale from her hospital bed the day after his birth. After just six weeks of maternity leave, Long was back at her desk wheeling and dealing again.

By the time her daughter was born a year and a half later, however, Long was exhausted. In addition to putting in face time every day from eight to five at the office, there were countless meetings she was expected to attend, plus the obligatory long evening hours schmoozing with clients. "As I held my new baby, I realized that I had missed the first one and a half years with Conor. In fact, he liked the baby-sitter better than me," she says. "And I decided that if I was going to continue working that hard, it was going to be for myself and my family."

In January of 1995, Long resigned her position and launched Connemara, Ltd., named for Conor and her daughter, Meaghan. Her firm, which she operates from the basement of her home in a suburb of Chicago, sells equipment to the utility industry. Connemara was an instant success, but within a year's time, Long was running herself ragged. "I was taking on more and more product lines—and part of me was thrilled," she says. "I kept saying to my husband, John, 'I'm doing fantastic!'"

But her moment of truth came the day she and John were supposed to be taking it easy at their Lake Geneva, Wisconsin, condo. "Our kids were bobbing in the water, and there we were—both with mobile phones at our ears," she recalls. "It was the silliest scene, and I turned to John and asked, 'What are we doing here?'"

Long subsequently mailed "Dear John" letters to most of her customers telling them she was dropping several lines. "They couldn't believe it," she reports. "One customer asked, 'Beth, what are you doing? You could make

$100,000 a year just on this one line!' But I knew that that $100,000 would also cost me ten hours a week of precious time with my husband and two children."

Long loves what she does and admits that it's a struggle every day to keep things balanced. "There's always a part of me that says, 'Go for the gusto. Why limit yourself?' Then I go back to thinking that when you're dying, no one ever says, 'Gee, I wish I had worked harder.'" In fact, time is increasingly precious to Long now that her oldest is in kindergarten and her youngest is a preschooler. "If I don't catch these few moments, pretty soon they'll be off to high school, and I'll have missed it," she says.

Friends still constantly remind her, "Beth, you could be a millionaire." But Long always responds by paraphrasing a quote—credited to the late Jacqueline Kennedy Onassis—that she says has become her personal mantra: "If you screw up raising your kids, nothing much else you do in life matters."

WHEN FLEXIBILITY SPELLS FREEDOM

Magda Nassar's career at AT&T was going great when she decided to plateau. In 1987, she was promoted to management and had two children while continuing to work full-time. "I took only six weeks off when my son was born and three months when my daughter was born," she says. "But as my kids grew older—they're now eleven and fifteen—I felt it was important to be there when they got home from school."

The trouble is, part-time managers were practically nonexistent at Bell Labs in 1990. "When I decided to switch from full-time to part-time, I told my boss I would step down as supervisor," Nassar recalls. "To my surprise, he suggested we try to work out a schedule that would satisfy my needs as well as the company's." The result: Nassar, forty-three, now works four days a week from 8:00 A.M. to 3:30 P.M., and on a fifth, floating day, stays until 6:00 P.M. "That enables me to attend afternoon business meetings," she explains.

This flexible schedule meant taking a cut in salary to reflect her part-time hours. Nassar also agreed to remain easily accessible—by phone, fax, and e-mail—to her staff while at home. "Initially, I hired a baby-sitter as well, who was on call in case something came up at work that required me to change the day I worked late at the last minute," she adds.

Since negotiating this schedule, Nassar hasn't been promoted again. "Last year, I was offered a new position that would have required a daily commute of about an hour and a half each way. But I had to turn it down because I didn't think it'd be possible to commute and hang on to my flexible work schedule," she says.

Nassar adds that it's not easy watching her peers—and even people who used to work for her—move up the ladder while she marches in place. "I struggle with that every day," she admits. "But for now, flexibility is more precious to me than advancement."

A JOB HUNTER'S MARKET

Nassar and others in the corporate world who have plateaued on purpose believe that corporate America is becoming much more open to flexible working arrangements. "I was too quick to assume that I would have to give up my position in management to work part-time," she says. "I think people are unnecessarily apprehensive about speaking up and asking for what they want and need." Indeed, with unemployment low and employee turnover at its highest in a decade, companies who want to hang on to experienced workers like Nassar have little choice but to come up with incentives like flexible hours.

John Challenger, executive vice president of the Illinois-based outplacement firm Challenger, Gray and Christmas, agrees. "In order to compete for employees, employers will have to up the ante. What used to be considered perks will become standard." Already, unprecedented numbers of companies are offering perks such as flexible work schedules, job sharing, and part-time options—and, thus far, results are encouraging for both sides of the equation. For example, until opening its Office for Retention in 1996, the Atlanta accounting firm Ernst & Young was experiencing heavy turnover—especially among women. "There were a lot of talented people we didn't want to see go out the door," says Deborah Holmes, who heads the Office for Retention. "And since we began offering flexible schedules, more than one hundred employees have signed up for it."

One of these employees is Wendy Vocelka, an executive with thirteen years' experience at the firm. She now works from 6:00 A.M. to 1:00 P.M., overseeing a staff of ten who audit benefit plans for clients throughout the Southeast. The rest of the day she is home with her four-and-a-half-year-old son Drew and thirteen-month-old triplets Amanda, Katherine, and Noelle. "My career is such an important part of what I am in my life," says Vocelka. "By them being flexible and helping me work through this part of my career, it helps me stay where I want to be."

ARE THERE PENALTIES FOR PLATEAUING?

Despite the widespread availability of flexible work schedules, job sharing, and part-time options, many employees are reluctant to take advantage of these benefits. "Family-friendly policies are wonderful, but they are underutilized. Men hardly ask for them, and if they do, they're seen as wimps," confirms Lottie Bailyn, Ph.D., professor of management at M.I.T.'s Sloan School of Management. "And if women take them, they're often put on the Mommy Track."

"That used to be the feeling at Xerox," reports Jill Allen, a marketing support manager for the company's Customer Administrative Center in Lewisville, Texas. "Behind any request for flexibility was fear of appearing less committed if you used a program that was ostensibly there to help you find better balance," she explains. "Yet, workers were not necessarily more productive just because they were there."

Xerox was one of three companies to recently take part in a groundbreaking four-year study by the Ford Foundation that examined obstacles to productivity at firms known for their work-life initiatives. "We found that the answers didn't lie in better policies and programs," says Bailyn, a member of the Xerox research team. "The ones in place were wonderful at these companies, but they weren't being used. We believed that if employers put family, community, and personal life upfront, they could restructure work in a way that not only addressed employees' concerns, but also helped the organization achieve its business goals."

"Employees clearly wanted to use the flexibility options we offered—but without being penalized," adds Allen. "Consequently, we have changed the environment so that people and teams are empowered to make the decision to be flexible, as long as business needs are met. Managers still establish boundaries, but they're far less rigid." As a result of this research, the number of employees on nontraditional schedules at the Lewisville Center has leapfrogged from 2 percent to 85 percent. Moreover, absenteeism has been slashed in half.

Researchers hope that the Ford Foundation study— the first of its kind—will serve as a model for other leading U.S. employers on how to make work-family benefits a win-win situation.

AN UNEXPECTED DEMOTION

Stephanie Hood, a seventeen-year veteran at DuPont, has similar hopes. Two years ago, she elected to plateau indefinitely while she raised two young daughters. Subsequently, she has paid dearly for her decision. "I had my first child in 1991 and went back to work full-time after a six-month leave," says the forty-year-old competitive intelligence manager for Dacron, a strategic business unit within DuPont. "In fact, there was a promotion waiting for me when I returned from maternity leave."

In 1993, seven months pregnant with her second child, Hood was offered another promotion. "This was a job that involved frequent trips to Asia, and at the time, I was clueless about how much more challenging it would be to juggle two kids and a job. So I accepted the position," she says. A year into it, however, Hood felt burned out. Seeking more balance in her life, she proposed cutting back to thirty hours a week, and that arrangement worked for a year. "To get the work done, however, I was putting in more than thirty hours, and my stress level skyrocketed. So I asked to switch jobs and was even prepared to leave the company if I had to."

That's when the trouble started for Hood. "My request was perceived by some as a weakness," she explains. And while Hood was able to keep her thirty-hour-per-week schedule and land a special assignment with less travel, her stress level continued to climb. "The project I was working on failed, then I was later bounced around to different positions in an effort to keep my flexible schedule," she says. A year ago, Hood was demoted. "I was taken down a full level, which meant no cut in salary at the time, because it put me in the top pay range of the lower level position," she says. "But money was never the issue anyway."

What bothered Hood most was the message the company was sending to others who hoped to follow her lead. "People's lives change, their goals change, and their values shift," she believes. "And companies need to understand that. Upper management obviously had a path in mind for me, and when I said I didn't want that path—at least not now—they couldn't think of me in any other way. Yet, I was someone in whom they'd invested fifteen years. Additional promotions weren't necessary. I was perfectly willing to plateau."

Hood has since adjusted to her new job and now works a full-time flexible schedule. "I get my forty hours in, but I'm also home by three-thirty to meet my kids when they get off the school bus." And while her current boss keeps telling her, "We need to move you on and up," Hood's response is, "Don't talk to me about that; this is perfect for me right now."

In many ways, Hood—who often gets calls from others, both inside and outside the company, who are considering plateauing—relishes her role as a trailblazer at

DuPont. "There were women ahead of me, who made it possible for me to advance as far as I have," she figures. "So, hopefully, hanging in there and fighting for what I believe is important will benefit the next generation. In fact, people I run into at work are always asking me, 'Are you still working flexible hours?' and they're so relieved when I answer yes. 'Good for you. I wouldn't have the guts to do what you've done,' they tell me. Then, typically, they ask me how my kids are doing. People envy me for my flexible schedule," she adds, "but it's not as easy as it looks—especially when the people who once worked below me are moving up to my level or climbing ahead of me. Sometimes that's a bit too much to swallow, but I haven't yet questioned what I've done."

For most women, plateauing is only a temporary move. And the good news is, it doesn't necessarily mean the kiss of death for a promising career. At Atlanta's Ernst & Young, for example, four people who use flexible work arrangements have been promoted to partner last year alone.

SUCCESS ON THEIR OWN TERMS AND TIMETABLE

Granted, sometimes careers may stall in the process of plateauing, but that, too, should only be temporary. Many predict that Ann Fudge will be the first black female CEO of a Fortune 500 company. At forty-six, she is already president of Maxwell House. But she's taken a roundabout way to get to the top and has clearly found success on her own terms.

Back in 1977—just after graduation from business school—Fudge set a personal goal of becoming a general manager by age forty. But her family always came first. "Because they were my first priority, career decisions were fairly easy," says Fudge, who from day one has acted without apology for being both an ambitious career woman and a mother.

In 1986, Fudge was on track for a big promotion at General Mills but decided to leave the company. Staying put could have meant reaching her goal well ahead of her game plan, and leaving could easily have meant falling off the fast track. Nevertheless, Fudge elected to accept another position in the Midwest working for General Foods. Her reasoning: it offered her the chance to be closer to her ailing mother, who lived on the East Coast. "In the end, it turned out to be the right decision, anyway," she says, "since there were many more opportunities to move up at General Foods."

A few years later came another offer for a major position in another city. "I declined again," says Fudge. "It would have meant relocating just as my son was entering high school. I didn't think it would be right to move him that year. And I didn't want to be a commuter wife and mom." Despite her decision to plateau—not once, but several times in her career—Fudge met her goal of being general manager by age thirty-nine and is now well on her way to making history.

Ruth Simmons *did* make history when she was installed as the ninth president of Smith College in September 1994. But on the way to being the first black woman tapped to head one of the elite "Seven Sisters" women's colleges, Simmons, too, found success on her own terms and timetable.

Now fifty-one, Simmons grew up in rural poverty, the youngest of a dozen children born to Texas sharecroppers. Despite being surrounded by rampant segregation, her parents always encouraged her to shoot for the stars. "The conditioning I got when I was a child was to not do anything unless you tried to do it at the best possible level," she says.

It was a lesson Simmons learned well. She attended college at Dillard University in New Orleans. She won a prestigious Fulbright Grant and studied for a year in France. Upon returning to the United States, she went on to Harvard University, where she received both her master's and doctorate in Romance languages. In 1985, Simmons was asked to direct the African-American studies program at Princeton University. Her efforts to revitalize that program have since become legendary, as she was instrumental in attracting such faculty as Cornel West and novelist Toni Morrison.

Yet, from the start of her career, Simmons was determined to keep family as a top priority. Picking up her young daughter from school every afternoon, for example, was of utmost importance to this divorced mother of two. And she made sure her colleagues and superiors at Princeton knew it—even if it meant she'd be late for a meeting, or miss it altogether. "My solution to balancing career and family was to make flexible hours a job requirement," she says. "And if a position didn't offer it, I'd find another one." This steadfast commitment to family did place Simmons on the slow track for a while, she acknowledges. But she was never too worried, and, in fact, with her latest achievement, has ended up having the last laugh. "Remember, women live much longer—their careers are much longer," she says. "It is entirely possible when you are in your late forties to take off in a career that's fabulous."

CHAPTER SIX

Backtracking: You Can Go Home Again

Far away there in the sunshine are my highest aspirations. I may not reach them, but I can look up and see their beauty, believe in them, and try to follow them.

—LOUISA MAY ALCOTT

Laura Brogden calls it the "no that saved her soul." In fact, the minute she said "yes" to a promotion two years ago, the thirty-four-year-old educational administrator from Port Angeles, Washington, knew it was a mistake. "But it was too late to take it back," she recalls. "I told myself all the reasons I couldn't turn it down: 'it's a great opportunity; a high-profile program that could propel your career. The extra money would really help. You deserve it; you *earned* it.'"

Fear also influenced her decision to accept the offer. "If you don't accept this promotion, you may never get another chance to move up," she rationalized to herself. "Turn down a promotion now, and you'll stay in this job forever." Besides, her family had offered their full support. "My husband was willing and able to do more at home," she reports. "I could spend extra time at work guilt-free, because I knew my young daughter was always with someone who loved her—her dad, her grandmother, or her aunt who had chosen home day care as her profession."

Initially, Brogden felt charged up by her new position. "The adrenaline was really flowing," she remembers. "I was making important decisions and proving my value to the institution I worked for. It was a natural step in my career." Things were going equally well on the home front. "I would rush home, exhausted—yet still ready to throw something together for dinner for my family, only to find them fed, bathed, and fine without me. I would hold my daughter in my arms and ask her about her day. And to both my dismay and delight, she didn't always miss me."

Exhausting work days, however, soon began to take their toll. "The more I achieved at work, the harder it became to hold on to it," Brogden says. "There was always something waiting, something undone. Gradually, I found myself working twelve-hour days. I missed my niece's first birthday party. I missed a friend's wedding and a family baby shower. 'This is investment time,' I kept telling myself. 'I won't always be this busy. Chin up!'"

Slowly but surely, Brogden began ignoring the rest of her life: her garden, her kitchen, her friends, and her writing. "Gradually, I had allowed my job to consume every moment of my life," she admits.

On the plus side, her dedication to her work had not gone unnoticed. "I was receiving compliment after compliment on my achievements," she reports. But kudos weren't enough. Inside, Brogden was miserable. "I grieved for unwatered plants, unwritten poems, unread books, and games left unplayed with my daughter," she says. "Still, I numbed my feelings and went to work. 'You can have it all,' I tried to convince myself. 'Look how well things are going at work. Look how well your family has adjusted at home.'"

The trouble was, Brogden herself was not adjusting so well to a life that had become dangerously one-sided. Consequently, she did the unthinkable by resigning from her promotion and asking to return to her old job. "The minute I did it, relief washed over me, followed by joy."

Not surprisingly, Brogden's boss had a radically different reaction—one of disbelief. He quickly reminded her of how well she was doing on the job and how well her family was doing without her. "What he didn't get—and couldn't understand—was that my decision wasn't about my family needing me," she says. "It was about me needing me, and me needing them. I wanted to be the one who cooked dinner, because I love to cook. I wanted to weed and water the garden—not because my husband couldn't do it, but because it gave me joy. And I wanted to be around to bathe my daughter, teach her things, and take her places."

In retrospect, Brogden acknowledges that her decision to backtrack may have ultimately ruined her career. But she's not concerned. "I've decided I can live with that risk," she insists, "because it was a decision, I believe, that saved my soul."

MOVING UP SPELLS SUCCESS

It's natural for women to equate success with moving as far up the career ladder as possible—and usually the quicker, the better. But many, once having landed at or near the top, feel overwhelmed and disillusioned. Consequently, they elect to move back down the ladder a notch or two and replace their exhausting and all-consuming careers with positions offering less pressure, lower visibility, and greater personal satisfaction.

The problem with backtracking is that it can often feel like failure. Moreover, when women willingly take a step backward in their fields—particularly male-dominated ones—a backlash frequently follows. After all, such a move seems to legitimize the stereotype that women don't have what it takes to make it at the top.

Three years ago, for example, forty-five-year-old Janet Daley, M.D., was tapped to head up the radiology department of a mid-sized teaching hospital in the Northeast. "I was elated to land the promotion and gung-ho to do an outstanding job," she says. Daley's appointment was especially applauded by the female staff of the hospital, where promotions of women to plum positions were few and far between. But after only two and a half years on the job, she decided to step down and resume her old position as a staff radiologist. "Both my work and my husband's career were going full-steam," she explains. "I felt that if we both continued putting in the hours we were working, something was going to fall apart. And frankly, I worried that it was going to be our marriage."

Before handing in her resignation, Daley debated the decision in her head—and heart—hundreds of times. "I had campaigned hard for that job and felt that by throwing in the towel, I had failed somehow. In fact, I had to keep reminding myself of how much I'd accomplished and how much I'd grown in the position," she says.

Had Daley had children at home, she feels it might have been easier to justify her decision to backtrack. "Probably people would have been more understanding and supportive," she notes. Instead, her resignation caused an uproar—especially among the hospital's female staffers. "Many pointed a finger at me, claiming I exacerbated the myth that women can't cut it at the top," she says. "Many also claimed I'd ruined *their* chances of being promoted. But I had to do what was best for me. And I'm entirely at peace with my decision."

DEALING WITH SMALLER PAYCHECKS

Pulling back, of course, also requires making sacrifices—particularly financial ones. But in terms of pure monetary and lifestyle impact, women who have backtracked tend to agree that the sacrifices required are not only surprisingly minimal, but well worth it.

When Beth McCarty gave up practicing law in 1991, her paycheck was slashed in half. "The initial cut was traumatic," says the forty-one-year-old former attorney, who lives in Chicago. "But I quickly recovered financially, and overall, I have to say that my lifestyle didn't change all that much." A 1983 graduate of the University of Wisconsin School of Law, McCarty chose corporate law as her specialty, but deliberately avoided being recruited by a huge firm. "I didn't want killer hours, so I chose a medium-sized firm to work for," she says. Unfortunately, three years into her career, that firm fell apart, and McCarty and several other colleagues moved to a larger firm in Chicago. For the next three years, she worked in corporate litigation, but after working on a pair of back-to-back trials that stretched out over two years, she was exhausted. "I had a standing appointment every week to get a massage, just so I could sit up straight," she recalls. "And I began thinking, 'This is definitely not something I want to do for the next forty years.' The thrill and joy of practicing law had vanished."

Before calling it quits, however, McCarty shopped around for a new career. "A former client of mine, Bonnie Michaels, had launched a new company called Managing Work and Family, and she needed some help. I liked what she was doing and decided to buy into the business as a principal." After two years of consulting with Michaels on work and life topics, McCarty was recruited to start up the Chicago office of The Partnership Group, now part of Ceridian Performance Partners. She led the team that created the award-winning Marriott's Associate Resource Line, helping lower-income workers manage their midlife challenges. "Being able to make a difference for people was why I went into law in the first place," she says. "And finally, I'd found a way to actually do that."

Today, McCarty is vice president for corporate accounts for Ceridian, a company that works with a variety of clients nationwide to help them develop workforce effectiveness programs, including LifeBalance, a resources and support service for employees. Her staff focuses on clients with more than eight thousand employees.

Meanwhile, McCarty has perfected a life-balance program of her own. "I still work hard, but unlike the law office I came from, this is such a collegiate and positive atmosphere," she reports. "Because of what we do, there's naturally a lot of flexibility in this position. Now I have time to fix up my house, putter in the garden, do a lot more volunteer work, and travel. I spent a month in Australia in 1995 and explored South America for nearly three weeks this year—significant periods of time off that would have never been possible before. In essence, I really enjoy what I do now. It's a heck of a lot easier to get up in the morning and look forward to the day ahead. Plus, I haven't needed a massage in six months!"

YOU CAN GO HOME AGAIN

For some women, backtracking is seen as a permanent move. For many others, however, it's a way to regroup, rebalance, and simply catch one's breath. Interestingly enough, such a drastic move doesn't always damage one's career. In fact, in many cases, these women's careers have prospered.

Marilyn Baxter, for example, has sailed in and out of her career as an advertising executive—not once, but twice—and still managed to land on her feet. In 1981, Baxter was working as a strategic planner for McCann Erickson in London when her longtime boyfriend, Martin Smith, then a government economist, proposed a two-year trip across the Atlantic on his sailboat. Baxter knew that saying yes to his pitch would mean saying bon voyage to her job. "But I felt I had been successful at Mc-Cann and could hopefully get another job in advertising when I returned."

Indeed, two years later, Baxter had barely unpacked before finding a job at Grandfield Rork Collins, a new agency cofounded by her former boss. Named deputy planning director, her title—and salary—were far better than the ones she'd left behind. Moreover, following a subsequent buyout of Grandfield Rork by Saatchi and Saatchi, Baxter was named planning director of the new agency.

Meanwhile, she and Martin dreamed of sailing the Pacific and decided to do just that in September of 1993. "We had a lot of loud debates about the trade-offs that second time around that we didn't have the first time," she recalls. "We were both well-ensconced in our careers and at our peak earning capacity. But we also felt that if we didn't sail the Pacific then, something could get in the way, and we never would."

Back ashore again in 1995, Baxter began looking for work. It was only slightly tougher this time—in fact, within a week, Saatchi and Saatchi (in crisis following the ousting of Maurice and Charles Saatchi) called and asked her to take charge of client services. "I found it appallingly easy to walk back in and go to work," she says. And, in fact, Baxter credits her sailing experience with making her a sharper executive. "Whenever there was a problem on the boat, we had to deal with it quickly," she explains. "Now, at the agency, I am driven to find solutions rather than worry for too long about problems."

SEEKING SERENITY IN SILICON VALLEY

Deborah Coleman has always been a trailblazer. In 1981, she joined Apple Computers as manager of manufacturing operations. Six years later, at the age of thirty-four, she became the youngest chief financial officer in the Fortune 500. During her tenure, Apple's revenues more than doubled—from $1.9 billion in fiscal year 1986 to $4.1 billion in fiscal year 1988.

Silicon Valley's legendary long hours, however, eventually led to high blood pressure and excess weight gain for Coleman. "I remember asking myself, 'Do I want to be the best CFO in the business and have a heart attack by the time I'm forty?'" she says. "I decided that I could either wait until I was burned out or deal with the situation proactively." Coleman chose the latter and subsequently resigned her post, sold most of her stock, and took five months off, during which she mostly worked out and hung out. "Before my sabbatical, I didn't have time for friends or family or exercise," she says.

At the time, Coleman also hoped to serve as a role model for others by demonstrating that it was "all right for a successful person in a high-growth company to reduce the scope of her responsibilities to achieve greater personal balance." Instead, she was barraged with phone calls and letters from female executives who criticized her move. "The male executives I heard from applauded my decision," she notes. "But most women felt that what I did sent the wrong message: that women at the top can't take the pressure and need time off."

In 1990, Coleman returned to Apple thirty-five pounds lighter and with a new title: vice president of information systems and technology. Two years later, she accepted the position of vice president of operations at Tektronix and moved to Wilsonville, Oregon. Today, at forty-two, she's at the helm of Merix Corporation, a $70 million spin-off company of Tektronix that makes advanced electronic equipment.

HAVING HER CAKE AND EATING IT TOO

In 1982, Donna Goya was a personnel manager and rising star at Levi Strauss when she elected to cut her work schedule from five to three days a week and her responsibilities from five divisions to three. Colleagues were shocked at Goya's move. "Most couldn't believe I did it so I could spend more time with my three-year-old son and his big sister," she says. "They were sure I was committing career suicide."

Two years later, when her son started kindergarten, Goya returned to regular hours—*and* a promotion to director of personnel. "One of the first things I did upon my return was get to work on changing a lot of personnel policies to make them more family-friendly," she says. Thanks to Goya, Levi Strauss employees now enjoy more generous maternity leaves without fear of losing their jobs. They can also use their own sick time to care for ill children and other ailing relatives. Flexible work hours became an option as well, and policies were enacted to enable workers to tap into their accrued and unused sick time for personal reasons.

In other words, things have changed a lot since Goya took her leave, a move that she acknowledges could very well have permanently stalled her career. "But I truly believe that the most important thing in life is to keep your priorities straight," she says. "I took time off when I felt my children needed me most, and I have no regrets." Nor should she. Despite the interruption, Goya's career has flourished. In 1985, she was named a vice president of human resources and a year later was promoted to senior vice president, proving that you can, indeed, go home again.

CHAPTER SEVEN

The Joy Crisis: Caring for Our Souls

It isn't until you come to a spiritual understanding of who you are—not necessarily a religious feeling, but deep down, the spirit within—that you can begin to take control.

—OPRAH WINFREY

Shoya Zichy began her career as a high school teacher at a private school in Greenwich, Connecticut. It was a job she loved but didn't make much money at. Thus, when many of her friends began making big bucks in the corporate world, she felt a twinge of envy. "I wanted to see what it was all about," she says.

A family friend helped her land a job at *Institutional Investment*, a financial trade magazine. While interviewing Citibank's head of international private banking, she was offered—and accepted—a job as an international private banker herself. Citibank sent her to Asia for four years, where she lived in Hong Kong and "mined" the Philippines for new clients. That job led to a position with Merrill Lynch, where she was based in New York but lived a jet-setting life assisting foreign investors across the globe. Eventually, she landed at American Express Bank, and, by 1988, had climbed the ladder to vice president.

"But the corporate culture there was stifling," she reports. "There was so much politics and infighting going on." Worse, the female way of doing business wasn't appreciated nor accepted. "From the start, I was given some friendly advice: 'tame down the curly blond hair, and don't do anything to stand out'—which, for me, was difficult, since I tend to be a bit eccentric," she says. "In fact, that's always been one of my strengths."

When the bank reorganized in 1989, and Zichy learned that her international real estate division would be shifted to Joliet, Illinois, she decided to seize the opportunity to make a clean break. Moving to Rockport, Massachusetts, instead, she opted to take some time off and do some painting. "I had dabbled in art as a child, and it was something I'd always wanted to take up again," she says. "I figured a three- to six-month hiatus was all I needed."

Six months melted into five years, and although Zichy was able to earn a decent living as an artist—many of her customers were Wall Street cronies—she found her life growing "financially scary." She also craved more stimulation. "I wanted to be connected with the business world again," she says. "Oddly enough, I missed it."

In early 1995, Zichy returned to Manhattan and gradually launched a consulting business designed to help women whose career paths and experiences seemed hauntingly similar to her own. "For so long, I had assumed my experiences to be unique," she says. "But here were all these extremely talented women—women with

MBAs, women with a dozen or more years in, women with executive positions. They should have been on top of the world: instead, many of them were miserable."

Zichy began asking herself, "Why are so many of these brilliant women burning out?" Now she earns a living testing, counseling, and trying to help these women rearrange their lives so they can feel more balanced and fulfilled.

Another recent specialty of Zichy's involves using psychological tests—like the Myers-Briggs Inventory—to help women achieve greater satisfaction from their work and better balance in their lives. Her consulting business is still in its infancy, yet to date Zichy has counseled more than five hundred clients.

PUTTING AN END TO POSTPONING HAPPINESS

"There's trouble in the American workplace," confirms Jack Canfield, in his book *Heart at Work.* "Profits are up, but people are down." What gives? Experts speculate that far too many of us may be spending too much of our time *preparing* to live, when our goal really should be to enjoy the process of being alive *right now.*

Certainly, one major cause for America's current joy crisis—particularly among working women—is a shortage of time to enjoy being alive, and a lack of balance. On the plus side, growing numbers are beginning to recognize and address this problem. "Oriental philosophy teaches us that nothing in the universe can swing too far in one direction without eventually seeking balance," notes Barbara DeAngelis, Ph.D., in her book *Real Moments.* "We, as Americans, sense how out of balance we have gotten, and we are beginning to shift from a consciousness of self-indulgence to one of self-discovery. Whereas we once measured success in terms of status, wealth, and accomplishment, now we are beginning to measure it in terms of how happy we are and how much peace of mind we've achieved."

Another major missing link for many of today's workers may be a sense of meaning on the job, believes Harold Kushner, author of *When All You Ever Wanted Isn't Enough.* "The need for meaning isn't a biological one, nor a psychological one," he writes. "It is a spiritual need, an ultimate thirst of our souls." In a recent Yankelovich Partners survey of three hundred career women, 73 percent said, "My work defines who I am." So, perhaps there lies another cause of this joy crisis. As Howard Schechter points out in *Rekindling the Spirit at Work,* "Work needs to be an expression in the outer world of who we are in the inner world. When we do work that is separate from who we are, 'just to make a living,' we usually suffer."

Scores of women we encountered are beginning to recognize all this and are learning how to sort out what's really important to them from all the glitz and glitter. To them, redefining success means asking themselves time and time again, "Is this what I *really* want out of life?" It also means putting an end to postponing happiness and taking the time to smell the roses once in a while.

A DREAM JOB TURNS DISASTROUS

Eight years ago, when she was fresh out of college, Melissa Garland landed her dream job as a public relations specialist for a mid-sized electronics firm on the

West Coast. There she worked on small accounts with friendly clients and was home every night in time to prepare and eat dinner with her husband and two young children. But four year ago, Garland's job changed dramatically when her company merged with a larger firm and was subsequently acquired by a Japanese corporation. With the layoffs that followed, Garland considered herself lucky to hang on to her job.

However, her job wasn't fun anymore. "Suddenly, instead of being home at night, I was either working late or out of town, eating bad food, sleeping in strange beds, getting yelled at by unfriendly clients, and missing my husband and kids. It wasn't what I had planned." Yet, despite her unhappiness and disillusionment, Garland managed to rise through the ranks to become a vice president.

"I kept telling myself I should be thankful," she says. "But there was this huge price to pay for success. I bought into working long hours on evenings and weekends and cutting vacations short to meet deadlines. And not only did I see less and less of my family and friends, I couldn't read for pleasure anymore—just business. Nor could I meet someone for lunch just to gossip or play 'catch-up.' I only went to lunch for business."

A year and a half ago, on the verge of a nervous breakdown—and a divorce—Garland decided to exit the rat race and start her own small public relations firm. "To my surprise, it was almost an instant success," she reports. "Many of my early clients supported me by throwing business my way. I started out with a part-time secretary in a small rented office, and within nine months hired an assistant, a support staff of three, and moved to a suite of offices. But the best part about the business is that I finally have flexibility."

FROM MOVIE MOGUL TO MENTOR

At the age of seven, Mara Manus was living a privileged life when she had her first encounter with America's homeless. Dressed in her Sunday best, Manus and her mother were on their way to a marionette show in New York City when the little girl spotted some shabbily dressed men sleeping on a sidewalk grate. "I remember asking my mother, 'Who are those men?'" she recalls. "And she told me, 'They are lawyers and doctors—men just like your father. Only they've fallen on hard times.'"

Throughout her life, hard times have not been something Manus has had a lot of firsthand experience with. By the age of twenty-six, the Stanford University graduate was vice president of production at Universal Studios. Six years later, she'd climbed the ladder to senior vice president of production at Trans Pacific Films, where she oversaw such comedies as *Fletch* and *To Die For.* But two events would soon change her life's course.

First, Manus ran into an old friend from an equally privileged background. "He was working for an agency that provided low-income housing, and I was so touched by the passion he obviously felt for his work," she says. "I suddenly realized that I should be moved to tears by my work, too." Soon after that, Manus *was* moved to tears— literally—when she was thrown from a horse while riding on the beach in Malibu. The six months she spent recuperating in a full body cast was a pivotal time in her life, she recalls. "It's when I first realized that my work wasn't satisfying me on a deep level."

Following her recovery, a friend of Manus's took her for a tour of Chrysalis, a private, nonprofit organization on Los Angeles's Skid Row that is dedicated to finding permanent jobs for the poor and homeless. She signed

78

up as a volunteer right away and was instrumental in launching the organization's second location in Santa Monica. Soon she was also named to Chrysalis's board of directors.

In January of 1995, Manus decided to trade in her six-figure salary as a movie mogul to become Chrysalis's executive director. Since she has taken over, Chrysalis has opened a third branch office—this one in Hollywood—tripled its annual budget to $3.2 million, enlarged its staff from nineteen to forty, and expanded job placements from four hundred to eleven hundred a year. "It's enormously satisfying to be a woman running a business—and one that accomplishes as much as this one does," she says. "No money could ever buy that."

A LEGACY OF JOY

Katy Tartakoff chose her occupation at the age of ten when she picked up a camera for the first time. Later, she graduated from Colorado Women's College with a double major in art education and psychology. For several years she taught preschool and elementary school while moonlighting as a professional photographer. When her mother died in the late '70s, however, Tartakoff's career took on a whole new dimension. "I remember asking myself, 'What is my vision—my purpose in life? How can I best use my gifts to make a difference in the world?'"

The answer came to her while watching a pitch for St. Jude's Hospital featuring Danny and Marlo Thomas, along with the hundreds of sick children for whom they were raising money and providing medical care. "I was so moved that I knew I had to work with those kids," Tartakoff says.

Moving to Memphis was out of the question, so, instead, Tartakoff approached Children's Hospital in her hometown of Denver. "My intent was to offer my services as a portrait photographer to take pictures—at no charge—of kids with life-threatening illnesses," she says. The hospital was enthusiastic about the idea but wasn't set up to administer the kind of program Tartakoff had in mind. Nevertheless, they encouraged her to launch such a project on her own.

"I did so—and very blindly," she recalls. Yet, from the start, Tartakoff knew that The Children's Legacy was meant to be. "On the very day that I announced my ambitions to a friend, a client called to ask if I'd be willing to photograph her six-month-old daughter who was dying of a rare muscular disease," Tartakoff explains. "I took that as a sign that I was definitely on the right track."

What she didn't realize, however, was how big The Children's Legacy would grow. As word-of-mouth about Tartakoff's services spread throughout the region, her client roster grew, and volunteers flocked to help support her cause. Today, The Children's Legacy is run by two paid staff members and hundreds of devoted volunteers. Moreover, it is fully financed by membership organizations, including foundations, corporations, individuals, and local businesses.

Its thrust has also expanded. In addition to taking portraits of children with life-threatening illnesses—along with their families, if desired—The Children's Legacy offers innovative workshops using art, photography, and writing to help families cope with the devastating blow life has dealt them. "Families are our focus in these, because when children are sick, everyone close to them is affected," Tartakoff explains.

Therapeutic activities used so effectively in these

workshops are now being shared all over the world, and a new CD-ROM developed by The Children's Legacy is in the works for health care providers, teachers, and families nationwide. "We're not a support group, nor are we therapists," Tartakoff adds. "But by using art, photography, and writing in our workshops, we give these families an opportunity to express and share their feelings. We also provide these sick children with a chance to leave their stories behind. In essence, our mission is to celebrate life—no matter how short it may be."

SHE'S NO MATERIAL GIRL

In high school, Debra Esparza was voted "Most Likely to Succeed." Yet, it was at her ten-year high school reunion that she first realized she was experiencing a joy crisis. To her former classmates, Esparza had lived up to everyone's expectations and had become a shining success. Having earned her bachelor's degree in finance from the University of Southern California (USC), she'd subsequently worked her way up from bank teller to vice president and branch manager for Southern California Bank. But at age twenty-eight, she was also burned out.

"I had everything I'd ever wanted," she says. "But it wasn't enough. The more money I made, the more things I could buy, and the less satisfied I felt. Something inside of me felt all shriveled up. I felt I just couldn't do it anymore."

And so, Esparza quit her job, dipped into her savings, and spent several months soul searching. "I kept asking myself, 'What have you contributed? What are you going to be remembered for?' I wanted to make a difference."

Esparza eventually made the decision to return to her

alma mater for an MBA—but with a specialty in entrepreneurship in the nonprofit sector. "As a banker, I had done a lot of community work—chaired the Christmas parade, sat on committees to revitalize the town, etc.—and enjoyed it immensely," she reports. To foot the bill for her new endeavor, she sold her stocks, cashed in her IRA, and took out student loans.

Once enrolled, the emptiness Esparza had been feeling inside quickly subsided. "I got involved in USC's Young Entrepreneurs program, which teaches school kids how to start their own small businesses and awards seed money and grants," she explains. In fact, Esparza began as a volunteer mentor for the program, and just before graduating in 1992, became its paid director. "My paycheck was about $10,000 less than what I could have been making in banking with an MBA," she says. "Plus, I owed Uncle Sam about $25,000 in student loans. But I was happy."

By 1994, however, Esparza's job had shifted focus. "We began working less and less with children and more and more with small, adult-owned businesses in the area. Our mission was to help them grow and prosper," she reports. Positive response to her program's new focus soon led the university to create what's called the Business Expansion Network—which currently services eight hundred to one thousand local businesses—and Esparza was tapped to develop and seek funding for the new organization. She has since brought in $7.5 million from public and private sources to bankroll the program and oversees a staff of twenty, including interns. She has also built her salary back up to six figures.

Yet, despite her success, Esparza is toying with the idea of chucking it all once again. "I've slowly made my way back to an institutional setting, where I find the constraints a bit suffocating at times," she explains. "I yearn for those happy-go-lucky days, and I miss working with young entrepreneurs. In fact, I just may decide to break away and establish my own independent agency that caters to this niche."

Kids are important to Esparza, who is single and has no children of her own. "All my life—thanks to the encouragement of family, friends, and mentors—I was always convinced I had potential," she says. "And to be able to go to work every day and make that kind of difference in children's lives—now *that* would bring me real joy!"

HAPPY BEING A B+ PERSON

When Beverly Cutler was named a trial court judge for the state of Alaska, she was thrilled. Her father, a renowned attorney in Washington, D.C., who has served as general counsel for presidents Jimmy Carter and Bill Clinton, was equally ecstatic. In fact, he had even higher hopes for his daughter.

"Early on, Dad pushed me to become a federal judge," says the forty-eight-year-old divorced mother of four. "But I've never been interested in putting in those kinds of hours. And even though I have thousands of pages of legal briefs to read each week, and occasional lost weekends, I'm working government hours—more or less—in a job I find interesting and challenging. In essence, I'm comfortable and content with what I have and what I am—a B+ kind of person."

Cutler learned as early as law school that to be happy she needed to lead a balanced life. "I couldn't spend sixteen hours a day studying like everyone else," she recalls.

"To keep my stress levels in check, I had to spend some time getting physical, so I used to swim laps every day."

In fact, it was her need for balance that attracted Cutler to Alaska in the first place. "The environment here makes it easier to be more well-rounded," she says. "Lots of people come here not only to work, but to hunt, ski, and fish."

After twenty years as a judge, Cutler still makes time to work out at an indoor pool and to do some occasional cross-country skiing. But her real joy and passion these days is farming. "My house sits on two hundred twenty acres where, in our spare time, the kids and I—with the help of a farm hand—plant and harvest potatoes and hay crops. I'm happier out here on the farm than anywhere else," she says. "There's something very therapeutic about driving a tractor."

CONSTRUCTING HER OWN JOY

Carole Wright Brogdon began her career as an accountant—not so much because she enjoyed crunching numbers, but to prove a point. "Both of my older brothers were successful accountants, and being the only girl in the family, I wanted to show them I could do it, too," she says. She did it well, graduating magna cum laude from the University of West Florida in 1974, then landing a job at a small CPA firm in her hometown of Fort Walton Beach, Florida.

In 1977, she moved to Atlanta to work for a larger firm—Main, Lafrentz (which later became part of KPMG Peat Marwick). Five years later, one of Main's clients wooed her away to head up their accounting division. In 1989, she snagged the position of director of national accounting for the Arthritis Foundation. Within three years, however, Brogdon was putting in killer hours, and the joy of working in her field had vanished. "I didn't have anything more to prove, and I just didn't want to do it anymore," she recalls. Consequently, she resigned her position and continued to consult for the foundation while she figured out her next move.

"The answer came to me while having dinner with friends one night," she says. "I had really enjoyed renovating several of the homes I'd lived in, so I thought I might try my hand at home building." Since she was choosing a whole new career, Brogdon figured she may as well leave Atlanta as well. "My fiancé lived in Savannah, Georgia, and both of us were growing tired of our long-distance relationship. Plus, I was anxious to move closer to home—and back to the coast," she adds.

Today, Brogdon is a partner in Carole Construction Associates, a small firm headquartered just outside Savannah. "I mostly handle the business side, but I also get to pick out house plans for our spec homes, choose colors, and consult on designs, which satisfies my creative side. I get to wear blue jeans and boots to work as well."

After five years in the business, Brogdon says she works just as hard as she used to, but now her hours are more flexible. "There are some twelve-hour days," she admits, "but there are many three- and four-hour days, too. Plus, I really enjoy what I'm doing. Granted, I'm making only a decent living doing this, but overall, it doesn't compare with my old career. This is so much better."

TRAGEDY BEGETS JOY

In 1990, when she lost her mom, Naeemah Chike was already in a joy crisis. Oddly enough, however, that tragic event helped Chike turn her life around. "I realized that if there was something you wanted to do with your life, you needed to stop waiting and just do it," says Chike, who, after four years of contemplating the idea, finally decided to go back to school.

Working full-time as a supervisor for a mid-sized telecommunications company in the Southeast at the time, Chike initially took just one course at a time so she could hold on to her job. But when the company began downshifting, she feared, despite her nineteen years of service, that her position would be eliminated. So she pooled her savings, pension, and investment earnings and became a full-time student at Agnes Scott College.

Pursuing a degree in sociology, Chike hopes to work with African-American teenagers when she graduates. Meanwhile, she's reveling in the simple life of a college student. "I'm as happy as a pig in mud now, and I don't have half the money I used to make," she reports. A sense of joy has also returned to Chike's life. "Recently, while walking to class, I noticed everything was in bloom, and I just took it all in," she says. "It made me realize that when I made the decision to follow my heart, all kinds of peace came my way."

A SECOND CHANCE AT FINDING JOY

It seems fitting that Lucinda Bassett would write a book entitled *From Panic to Power*. After all, she spent the first twenty-odd years of her life engaged in a marathon joy crisis. "I was raised by alcoholic parents and suffered from severe anxiety, as well as an eating disorder," she reports. "And as I grew older, I became increasingly agoraphobic."

Somehow, Bassett managed to enroll in nursing school at Ohio State University and earn a 4.0 average. "It was a real struggle," she recalls. "I had trouble sitting still in class and often visited the emergency room of the local hospital for heart palpitations. I was afraid of everything, and what I really wanted most of all was to die. But I was afraid to do that as well."

Fortunately, Bassett's life took a turn for the better after she found a therapist who diagnosed her panic disorder. Salvation also came in the form of the man she would eventually marry. "David was very loving and very accepting of my condition. He was there to support me—without enabling me—and to catch me whenever I fell apart," she says. "He made a huge difference in my life."

The panic disorders expert Bassett hooked up with also turned out to be a godsend. "She recognized my potential and eventually hired me to lead seminars for groups of people suffering from anxiety," she says. That, in turn, led Bassett to create an entire program designed to attack anxiety, which is used today by major hospitals and therapists worldwide. This phenomenally successful program subsequently formed the basis of her best-selling book.

Seven years ago, Bassett also founded the Midwest Center for Stress and Anxiety in Oak Harbor, Ohio. A year later, David quit his job to help her run the center, and four years after that, the couple moved to Los Angeles with their two children and opened a second center.

"I get tremendous joy from what I do," says Bassett, who has never turned away anyone from her clinic who suffers from anxiety. "We've treated clients who literally live in their cars. After all I've been through, how could I say no to someone who is penniless but in pain?"

Not surprisingly, Bassett has had numerous opportunities to expand her successful program. "Last year, we were negotiating with a company that represented a huge hospital chain, but their pushy ways really turned me off," she says. "Each time we'd meet, I could feel the negative energy. In fact, once, when I tried to put my two cents in on how the program should be run, one of the negotiators looked me in the eye and said, 'Little lady, you need to think of us as an eight-hundred-pound gorilla, and yourself as nothing more than a flea'—at which point, I thanked them for their interest and ended the negotiations. Three months later, I wasn't surprised in the least to hear that that company had fallen apart."

Thanks to her exuberant personality, Bassett has also had two different offers to host tabloid-type TV talk shows—both with lucrative book deals attached. But she's walked away from these opportunities as well. "That's not where my heart is telling me to go," she explains. "I can't live my life chasing dollar signs, because, to me, true success is not about money."

Instead, Bassett's intentions are to focus on a different theme: second chances. "This was something I was given—and something that brought me unparalleled joy and peace," she says. "Now my mission is to make sure others have the opportunity to do the same."

PRACTICING WHAT SHE PREACHES

It figures that Carey Sipp would start a company called The Sane Mother®. A self-described "recovering workaholic and spendaholic," this forty-year-old divorced mother of two recently moved her family from a sprawling five-bedroom house in a tony Atlanta suburb to a more affordable condominium. Simultaneously, she cut her work hours to four six-hour days to be with her kids more and to manage her home more efficiently and effectively.

In addition to working as an independent contractor for Capital Publishing—which puts out three magazines, *American Benefactor, Worth,* and *Civilization*—Sipp is marketing a book, self-help tapes, and other products aimed at today's pressured moms, particularly single ones. "My aim is to become the Erma Bombeck for single mothers," says Sipp, who also speaks and leads workshops on this topic.

"I've turned my life upside-down and inside-out for the better," she believes, "and I have never felt greater joy or sanity. I am freeing myself from the urge to collect things in favor of collecting great memories with my kids—listening to my three-year-old name the worms she just dug up and watching my six-year-old laugh himself silly over our Cheerio-eating polliwogs."

FROM CEO TO PSYCHOLOGIST

In 1996, Mary Collins Shields was the envy of practically everyone in Colorado Springs. After all, she was barely in her forties and had already built—from scratch—one of the largest and most successful real estate agencies in the area. She served as president of a local organization dedicated to wiping out child abuse and sat on seven boards for other civic causes. A few years earlier, she had gone back to school to finish her bachelor's degree and was now commuting once a month to Santa Barbara, California, to pursue a master's degree in psychology. On the side, she operated a small private counseling practice, plus still managed to oversee the business side of her real estate company.

"I can't believe you can do it all," people would always remark to Shields. "And the more I heard that, the more things I tried to accomplish," she says. But inside, Shields says she was dying. "I began feeling very anxious, very irritable, and I was exhausted." At the suggestion of her therapist, Shields attended a week-long journaling workshop led by the renowned psychologist Jean Shinoda Bolen, author of *Goddesses in Every Woman*. There, thirty highly successful women from around the world shared their life stories and explored their feelings and identities.

"It changed my life," Shields reports. And by year's end—the very night that she received the prestigious Business Woman of the Year award for Colorado Springs—Shields made a shocking announcement. She had sold her real estate business and was moving to Carmel Valley, California, to lead a much quieter life.

Today, Shields and her husband are managing to get by on half the income they used to. "I'm now beginning to do the things I feel called to do—things that don't have other people driving them," she says.

Specifically, Shields is pursuing a doctorate in mythology and will be among the first of twenty-five individuals in the country to graduate with expertise in a new field called archetypal psychology. "This field explores the cultural myths we all—especially women—tend to unconsciously live out in our personal and business lives, and how doing so can not only affect our creative processes, but the decisions and choices we make in life," she explains.

Shields is simultaneously launching a small private practice that will teach women how to use interactive journaling to find and create their own mythology and make better decisions in their lives. "My passion now is to help women who have lost their way to find their way back home," she says. "For once, I'm doing something my heart is telling me to do. And I couldn't be happier."

THE BURNING QUESTION

Suppose you knew you were going to die tomorrow. How would you want to be remembered? That's the question Richard Capen, Jr., recently asked two hundred of the nation's top business and political leaders for the basis of his book *Finish Strong*.

If you're experiencing a joy crisis, we recommend asking yourself this same question. Doing so will not only help you sort out what's important to you personally, but should also spur you to brainstorm ways to restructure your life to make room for more joy. By all means, don't discount your past successes. Rather, think about ways to add new ones that focus less on the tangible and more on the fulfillment of values closest to your heart and soul.

Capen, a former ambassador to Spain, deputy assistant secretary of defense, and publisher of the *Miami Herald,* admits himself that his illustrious career had taught him that titles don't grant fulfillment. "I think there is a certain joy that money can't buy, that power can't buy," he says. "It comes from knowing you're doing the very best in your own little world to live out your values."

CHAPTER EIGHT

Boredom Not Burnout:
When the Thrill Is Gone

Life is either a daring adventure or nothing at all.

—HELEN KELLER

A dozen years ago, Brenda Casabona was working as an international economist for the Commerce Department in Washington, D.C., when she made a bold decision to change her life. With a major in political science and a master's degree in applied economics, Casabona's specialty was researching, writing, and reviewing policy reports for a variety of industries from steel to sugar. "But there was no visible result from what I did," she says. "And all around me, people were saying, 'Only ten more years until retirement.' It was depressing!"

On the side, in her spare time, Casabona had become interested in candymaking. "Initially, it was the chemistry of it all that appealed to me," she says. But the chocolate confections she created earned rave reviews from friends and family. "Everyone was always telling me

I should open my own shop," she reports. And when Casabona did just that in 1984, everyone thought she was insane to give up a secure job for something so risky.

Her venture turned out to be not so risky after all. Within three months of purchasing a defunct bakery in Vienna, Virginia, Casabona reopened as DeFluri's Decadent Desserts & Chocolates. And within five years, she moved to a new location down the street, doubling the size of her operation.

Today, following over a decade of success, Casabona is planning yet another move—this time to Martinsburg, West Virginia. "I'm getting out of the bakery business to focus solely on candymaking. Chocolate has always been my passion, and we've built up enough of a clientele to make a go of it selling our confections wholesale nationwide. We'll also continue to operate a small retail business on site and do some mail order." Having her own business, Casabona adds, has enabled her to recharge her life. "In my old career, I put in so much time and effort, but rarely saw any results—which wasn't very gratifying. But here, while I certainly don't always have control over everything, there's never a dull moment."

In her first four years in business, Casabona earned less than her economist's salary—plus she often worked a backbreaking one hundred hours per week. But she never complained. "The quality of my life soared," she insists. "Before that, I would often sit at my desk and think, 'Three more hours before I can go home.' But in my own business, there were lots of days when I'd look up at the clock and think, 'My god, five hours couldn't have passed!' And that *still* happens today!"

GOING WITH THE FLOW

By switching careers, Casabona was able to achieve what University of Chicago psychologist Mihaly Csikszentmihalyi, Ph.D., calls "flow," a state of mind so exhilarating and focused that time passes unnoticed. "Flow is what happens when we become so totally involved in what we're doing that the external world seems to melt away," he explains. "It's a primary source of pleasure and self-esteem, and it's most likely to happen not only in the midst of a goal-oriented activity, but when one's skills match the challenges at hand."

Satisfying work is one of the best ways people can achieve this high, Csikszentmihalyi adds. "But it won't happen without your participation. You have to ask yourself what you want from life and how you can find a job that's at least, in part, expressive of your own best abilities."

TAKE THIS JOB . . .

Casabona is but one prime example of women who are redefining success by trading in mindless, unfulfilling jobs for more meaningful work. In a recent Yankelovich Partners survey commissioned by *Fortune* magazine, researchers found that job satisfaction among managerial and executive women peaks at about age forty—with 42 percent of respondents ages forty to forty-four agreeing that they are becoming bored with their jobs.

"Dissatisfaction appears to be especially widespread among people in their thirties and older," adds Pamela Pagliochini, a New York City–based, nationally certified career counselor. And the reasons for this discontent?

Pagliochini suspects it may be because many baby boomers chose their careers haphazardly to begin with. "We grew up hearing our Depression-era parents talk about work solely as a way to earn a living," she explains. "But we all have the potential to feel satisfied with our careers. Being happy in our work is a fundamental choice—much like being in a happy relationship."

It takes vision, guts, and enormous confidence to make a radical lifestyle change—particularly at midlife. But, like Casabona, those who've done it wholeheartedly agree that getting a fresh start on a new career can literally transform your life . . .

THE DIFFERENCE BETWEEN WALKING AND DANCING

Books have always been a big part of Lisa Von Drasek's life, but she never realized the depth of her passion until she went from peddling books to lending them. "The difference is like that between walking and dancing," she says. Von Drasek began her career in sales, working first for Putnam Publishing, then William Morrow, and finally for a consulting firm that served a variety of publishing giants. "But when you sell thousands of books, you don't really change anything," she says. "I didn't want to be Mother Teresa, but I thought, 'There's got to be more than getting up in the morning and putting together sales figures.'"

There was, she soon discovered after meeting a librarian who encouraged Von Drasek to switch fields—and even consider going back to school for a degree in library science. Her mentor also told Von Drasek of an opening for a children's librarian at the Brooklyn Public Library and gave her the director of personnel's name to call for an interview. "I had always berated myself for devouring children's books and young adult novels, but it never dawned on me that I might make a good librarian," she says.

Still, she hedged on making a career switch—until a coincidence motivated her to take action. "I happened to turn on the public radio station I normally listen to, and interestingly enough, the guest speaker on *Talk of the Nation* was the president of the American Library Association," Von Drasek recalls. "She gave a very motivating speech about the importance of libraries in our country, and I took that as a sign that perhaps this *was* what I was meant to be."

Von Drasek landed the job at the Brooklyn Public Library and simultaneously began a three-year, part-time master's degree program in library science. "Financially, it was a struggle. But my husband was very supportive, and I loved what I was doing." In addition to working with undereducated teenage moms striving to read, as well as recent immigrants eager to become literate citizens, Von Drasek developed a successful writing program that was quickly adopted by sixty other branches. "The kids would always run up to my desk and ask, 'When are we going to write?'" she says. "And that made me feel like I was making a difference."

Five years into her job at the Brooklyn Public Library, Von Drasek was promoted to senior librarian. "Finally, I was earning close to what I'd made before leaving the publishing world," she says. "I also had seniority, a pension plan, and job security for life." Nevertheless, a classified ad in the *New York Times* for a librarian's position at the Bank Street College of Education caught her eye, and despite the fact that the position was only guaranteed for a year, Von Drasek decided to go for it. "I think sometimes you have to take chances and have faith that everything will work out," she says.

In her new position, Von Drasek works with graduate students at Bank Street College who plan to become teachers, as well as with her first love—children in grades K–8 who attend the college's lab school. "It's the best of both worlds," she says. "Every day I learn something new." In fact, thinking back to the speech she heard on the radio that spurred her career switch, Von Drasek remembers calling into that show to say she was thinking about giving up her publishing job to become a librarian. "They put me on the air, and after talking for a few minutes to the president of the American Library Association, she told me, 'You *must* do this. You'll never regret waking up in the morning and going to work,'" Von Drasek recalls. "And she was right."

WINDING UP INSTEAD OF WINDING DOWN

In the early '90s, Nancy Moses was the managing partner of a Philadelphia marketing communications company. Her firm was doing well—boasting at least a million dollars in gross sales annually. But she felt something was missing. Her job had lost its allure, and at midlife, she was feeling increasingly unchallenged and unfulfilled.

"A friend suggested that I attend an encounter workshop she'd heard glowing things about," Moses reports. "When I asked why, she insisted, 'What you'll walk away with is a clear sense of what you want out of life, and a community of people to help you get where you want to go. Plus, it'll stop you from bitching all the time!'"

The workshop, which stretched for forty hours over four days, was a "powerful experience," Moses reveals. "There were thirty of us in all—everyone from executives and psychologists to major-league ball players and artists. We laughed together, cried together, did some writing, and shared our stories. I left deciding to sell my interest in the firm and pursue work in my major at graduate school—in historic museum management."

After liquidating her share, Moses took a three-month sabbatical to check out what others in her field of training were doing. She then met with her close colleague the mayor of Philadelphia, who encouraged her to visit Colonial Williamsburg, Savannah, Georgia, and Ireland—all under the auspices of an ambassador of sorts for his office. "He basically gave me carte blanche to travel as a volunteer 'expert' in cultural tourism, and assuming that role opened a lot of doors for me," she says. Moses then served for several months—this time for pay—as a consultant to clients such as the National Park Service and the City of Philadelphia, a position which enabled her to attend a White House Conference on Tourism and Travel.

In 1995, a job opportunity came along that Moses couldn't resist. "The Atwater Kent, which is the City of Philadelphia's history museum, was looking for a director," she reports. "The job was five blocks from my house and didn't require much traveling. I knew the place was having financial problems, but when I said yes, I didn't know how bad things actually were. So, for a while, it was a case of ignorance is bliss."

Besides, Moses was confident that managing a museum would be just like running a business. "But it wasn't," she says now. "I was used to making decisions whose consequences would be felt for sixty days or sixty months, not sixty—or even one hundred and sixty—years." She was also forced to learn how to manage people in a different way. "I've got a dynamite staff and a terrific board of directors, but to get everyone working as a team, I had to recognize that people who work in nonprofits aren't generally in it for the money. You must inspire them in a different way, treat them like peers, and find ways to help them grow. By contrast, in the corporate world, the bottom line was always what mattered most."

Not surprisingly, Moses was able to turn things around at the museum in two years' time. "My first year, I focused on upgrading the staff, setting a strategic direction, organizing focus groups with prospective visitors, and raising money," she explains. Subsequently, the Atwater Kent's budget has increased by 58 percent—to $1.2 million. Visitor numbers are up as well, and an expansion is in the works.

"I wanted a big new challenge, and at this wonderful old museum, I've found more than one," says Moses. In fact, at forty-nine, she's delighted that her career has "opened like a daffodil. A lot of my friends are starting to wind down in their careers, but I'm winding up. It's time for me to make my mark, and this job is a perfect fit."

IN SEARCH OF A CHALLENGE

Ann Iverson was a twenty-one-year veteran at Ogilvy & Mather, one of New York's most prestigious advertising agencies, when she reached a crossroads. She had climbed the ladder to senior vice president and international group director, but discovered that the higher you go, the less often you get to focus on the work you love most. "When I started out in 1970, the emphasis was on creativity and innovation, which were my passions," she says. "But increasingly, the focus had become the bottom line. And frankly, I was bored."

In fact, Iverson's job entailed coming up with big ideas for clients, but she was having trouble coming up with big ideas for herself. "I felt stuck," she reports. "So finally, I signed up for a weekend career seminar in hopes of finding the tools to break out of what was becoming a very frustrating situation."

By the time the session wrapped up, Iverson realized that she wanted to work independently, and in September of 1991, she resigned her post at Ogilvy & Mather. Before hanging up her own shingle as a strategic marketing consultant, however, Iverson took a sabbatical. "I desperately needed to clear my head and make sure I was headed in the right direction."

During her sabbatical, Iverson took a cooking class in Italy and went hiking in the Canadian Rockies. Six months later, she was ready to launch her venture, which she began in New York, but soon moved to Houston, Texas. "My husband and I had lived there before, and we had both business and family connections in the area," she says. "Plus, the lifestyle was less expensive and more laid back in Houston than it was in Manhattan."

Initially, money was a concern for Iverson, who'd taken a substantial pay cut to establish her own firm—and still isn't making what she used to. But she has plenty of big-name clients—Exxon, Shell, and Cooper Industries, to name a few—and absolutely no regrets. "I love what I'm doing and find my work intellectually stimulating and extremely challenging," she says. "In fact, the greater the challenge, the better. I've taken on some major assignments with no resources whatsoever, yet still managed to pull it off. And that's an incredible feeling."

FROM STUDENT TO INSTRUCTOR

Three years ago, Andrea Heaney had a successful career as vice president of corporate banking at Manhattan's State Bank of South Australia. But at thirty-three, she was tired of her job. "I felt bored and depressed most of the time, and all too often at work, I found myself just going through the motions."

Heaney turned to a career counselor for help. "Amazingly, when she asked me what my favorite accomplishment was, I surprised even myself when I blurted out, 'Baking sixty dozen cookies for friends and family every Christmas.'"

Heaney worked with her counselor for nearly a year before deciding to take a course in basic French cooking to determine if food preparation really was her niche. She not only aced the course, she ended up resigning her position at the bank to become a professional chef, and now she herself teaches full-time at Peter Kump's New York Cooking School in Manhattan.

To pursue her new career, Heaney paid a price. "Initially, my paycheck was cut to a third. Now I'm making about two-thirds of what I used to, but the money's not worth it. Besides, the perks are better at this job." Indeed, Heaney recently had her first child and was able to take a four-month maternity leave. "At the bank, all I could have gotten was six weeks. Plus, my boss has given me flexible hours so I can adjust to motherhood and have more time to enjoy my daughter."

The accomplishments Heaney is most proud of these days have changed considerably. "I baked the pastries that were photographed for Nick Malgieri's most recent [his fourth] cookbook," she relays with pride. "This is definitely the best decision I have ever made. There's just no comparison between what I'm doing today and what I used to do. Now I wake up every single morning eager to earn—excuse the pun—my daily bread!"

CHAPTER NINE

Postpartum Blues:
Putting an End to the Tug-of-War

The work will wait while you show the child the rainbow, but the rainbow won't wait while you do the work.
— PATRICIA CLIFFORD

Former congresswoman Susan Molinari vividly recalls the day the ambassador from Bosnia came to her office for a meeting. "He was early, and I was busy cleaning disposable wipes off my desk when he arrived. He had to stumble over my daughter's Tickle Me Elmo doll, and there were still mushy graham crackers scattered on the floor. The place looked more like a day-care center than a congressional office," she writes in an article for *Family Circle* on why she left Congress.

A little over a year earlier, at age thirty-eight, Molinari had become a first-time mom. "I thought I was prepared for everything," she says. "I had read every book I could find on motherhood. At the time, my husband and I were both in Congress, representing districts on opposite ends of New York State and traveling between three different homes. We had three cribs, three strollers, and three high chairs. We'd even equipped each of our offices on Capitol Hill with changing tables."

What Molinari wasn't prepared for, however, were the pangs of guilt she felt spending long hours away from her daughter, Susan Ruby. "From the second you decide to have a child, you dream of the moment she looks up at you and says, 'Mama.' The trouble is, I didn't realize I would be hearing her even when we were apart. Her voice and face would creep into my thoughts in the middle of debates on how to balance the budget or whether to send troops into Bosnia," she says.

As her daughter continued to grow and develop, Molinari felt more and more torn. "I wanted more time with her, but I wasn't sure I could give up my political career," she recalls. Then, an unexpected job offer to co-anchor *CBS News Saturday Morning* came her way, and the communications major who'd always dreamed of a position in broadcast news decided to say yes.

But not without a lot of soul searching. After all, politics was in Molinari's blood, and she was afraid that by giving up her post, she'd be letting her family down. "My grandfather was a member of the New York Assembly. My father was a former congressman then serving as Staten Island borough president. Plus, my husband, Bill Paxon, was the congressman for Buffalo, New York."

Molinari also fretted about disappointing her constituents. After all, the enormously popular congresswoman had begun her political career at age twenty-eight, serving as the minority leader of the New York City Council. In 1996, she had been tapped to give the keynote speech for the Republican National Convention. Also, as the highest-ranking woman in the

House, she'd earned kudos for her accomplishments on behalf of women and children's rights, specifically pertaining to domestic violence and child abuse.

Nevertheless, Molinari decided that the opportunity to join CBS offered the best of all possible worlds. "I could remain involved in national affairs and pursue a lifelong passion," she says. "I would also have more predictable hours, allowing me more time with my daughter. . . . Life is too short not to cherish the special people in our lives. I never want to look back and regret having missed the best years of my daughter's life."

PUTTING FAMILY FIRST

Perhaps never is there a greater need for women to redefine success than when the work-family balance is thrown off kilter. A majority of mothers forced to work long hours and endure frequent travel quickly realize that something has to give. And for many, it's work.

Karen Sukin grew up in a traditional household. "My mother didn't work, but both my parents firmly believed that the women in our family should be well-educated," she says. "The rationale wasn't necessarily that my sisters and I should expect to work as professional adults, but that we would be capable of doing so should we choose or need to."

Sukin graduated from her Billings, Montana, high school as valedictorian of a class of six hundred. She elected to attend Brown University as an undergraduate. Examining her options her senior year, she took the LSATs—almost on a whim. Earning a near-perfect score and carrying a near-perfect GPA, she applied and was admitted to Harvard Law School. In 1989, with degree in hand and plenty of job offers, Sukin decided to accept a position at a large Atlanta law firm.

Enthusiastic about her career from day one, Sukin quickly became a valued player and progressed along the firm's partnership track. Her desire to have a family, though, was never out of her thoughts. After three years of practice and five years of marriage, she decided to get pregnant. "One proven course for combining success at a large firm with parenting was to wait to have children until after becoming a partner," she says. "But having children was too important to me to risk trying to get pregnant at an older age. I wanted to be a young mom like my mother had been."

Three months after the birth of her son, Sukin hired a nanny and returned to work full-time. "The lawyers with whom I worked were so very supportive. I was encouraged by my mentors to continue working full-time, but to leave early if I needed to. The idea was that I would not lose any respect and could continue on track untarnished," Sukin says. "That kind of support is hard to come by in the field of law, but my team at the firm really wanted to see me advance."

Sukin felt guilty slipping out early, however, and soon voluntarily negotiated a forty-hour work week with the firm (which was about 75 percent of her full-time hours), so she could justify leaving the office in time to get home for dinner. When her daughter was born a year and a half later, Sukin remembers doing some serious soul searching. "I had a great nanny and very happy children, so it was easy—logistically speaking—to leave them. But I wasn't happy delegating my parental role," she recalls.

Still, Sukin loved her job and decided to pitch another proposal to the firm. "I offered to reduce my time at work from 75 percent to 60 percent, and they accepted my idea—which, again, was very unusual. I was fortunate to be of enough value to the firm for them to be willing to do this for me."

This arrangement, however, required that Sukin had no choice but to step off the partnership track. "That was acceptable to me, because I realized that making partner would take a tremendous amount of time and energy over the next few years separate from the regular practice of law. With young children at home, I wasn't sure the time was right for me to be making that commitment to my career," she says. "So, initially, I felt almost relieved by the agreement. And I felt confident that I would be brought back on track when I was ready to increase my commitment to the firm."

In July of 1996, six months after giving birth to her third child, Sukin opted to become a full-time mother and leave her job altogether. "The firm really wanted me to stay on and was disappointed by my decision," she says. "Even though I was working a reduced schedule, I had continued to be promoted by the firm. At the time I made the decision to leave, my team was starting the wheels turning for another significant promotion. But I saw a slippery slope ahead. I knew that after I earned the new title they wanted for me, I would feel compelled to stay on while my children's early years quickly passed. I also felt an obligation to other women looking to me as a role model—one of the first and few to successfully negotiate part-time as an associate. If I was given the new position and then left, I felt I would let those women down. Nagging at me, too, was the fact that while I really enjoyed practicing law, continuing to do so felt selfish. After all, the money—after child-care ex-

penses and taxes—was not making a significant contribution to our lifestyle."

Besides, with a third child at home, the tug-of-war
Sukin had felt after the birth of each child was intensify-
ing. "At home, I would be thinking about work," she says,
"and at work, I would be thinking about my children. I
was traveling between work and home—physically and
emotionally—several times each day. Making that transi-
tion between the two was definitely getting tougher."

Today, Sukin's days are spent playing with, loving,
reading to, and talking with her brood—plus carting
them to and from piano lessons, karate, religious school,
soccer, and ballet. "I'm very busy," she says. "I vividly remember the pressures of work, of being responsible for
the financial well-being of others. It is hard enough to
get three young children ready for their days each morning. If I were working, I'm afraid I'd be out of patience
with them in the morning because I'd be anxious to get
to the office for a conference call or a meeting. I'm relieved that I don't have that kind of stress in my life."

Still, Sukin says she misses the adult company work
used to offer and admits to living vicariously through her
husband—also a lawyer—at times. "It's hard to be the
wife at lawyer get-togethers," she confesses. "And while I
get a lot of praise for what I'm doing, it's also difficult to
remember that it's not meant to be condescending."

Sukin says she also sometimes worries that by not tot-
ing a briefcase off to work each morning, she's not the
role model she thought she'd be for her youngsters. "I
don't want my children to grow up thinking it is only a
daddy's job to go to work and make money," she says.
"But I also think it is important that they know it is okay
for a woman to choose to stay home with her children."

Sukin manages to stay current in her field by reading

journals, taking occasional courses to keep her certification up to date, and surfing the Internet's many law-related Web sites. As far as returning to work once her children get older, Sukin is taking a wait-and-see attitude for now. "I'm not making any specific projections," she says. "For the moment, I'm just doing what I think is in my children's best interest. And thus far, my choices have been right for me."

Not to say that resigning one's job is a necessity. On the contrary, never before have there been so many options available to both women and men who crave the time and energy to enjoy parenthood without sacrificing their careers. And in fact, both sexes appear to be taking advantage of these opportunities. For example, in a 1995 survey of more than six thousand employees at DuPont, nearly half the women and almost as many men had traded career advancement to remain in jobs that gave them more family time. "What people really want is to be both good parents and good at work," says Fran Rodgers, CEO of Work/Family Directions in Boston. And growing numbers are managing to do just that.

EXITING THE BIG CITY FOR A SLOWER PACE OF LIFE

In 1995, Cindy Brams, a thirty-one-year-old mother of two, was thrilled to land a job as finance director of a large Atlanta hospital. The salary it paid was more than she'd ever dreamed of making and would go a long way in helping her family live well in the big city. But within two years, Brams was miserable. "The work was challenging, but the hours were grueling," she explains. "My boss expected me to be at her beck and call round-the-clock, which really cut into my family time. In essence, it felt as if I'd sold my soul for a lot of money—and it definitely wasn't worth it."

In fact, the turning point for Brams came at the end of an eleven-hour work day in 1997 when her husband, Joey, was out of town. "I was on my way out the door to pick up my children from day care when my boss stopped me and said I had to stay late to put together some figures for a meeting the next morning," she recalls. Brams was irritated but quickly called a friend and arranged for her kids to be picked up.

At 10:30 that night, Brams finally finished her work and went to retrieve her children. "Both were sound asleep, and my friend helped me carry them to the car," she says. "Once home, I couldn't rouse either of them, and I was afraid to leave one in the parking lot alone." Instead, she carried them both—her four-year-old flung over her shoulder and her two-year-old in her arms—up two flights of stairs to their beds. Brams then collapsed on the sofa and burst into tears. "Why am I doing this?" she wondered aloud.

The following day, she expected to feel better after a decent night's sleep. Instead, the first thing she heard upon arriving at work was that the meeting that had caused her to work late the night before had been canceled. "I wanted to cry all over again," she says. "Clearly it was time to make a change." Within a month, Brams had decided to resign.

Immediately after giving notice at work, Brams's stress levels plummeted—until she called the local recreation department to sign her oldest son up to play soccer. "The woman who answered told me there were only enough facilities to accommodate a certain number of players Ben's age," she reports. "And my best bet for assuring him a spot on a team? She advised me to do what many other parents had done for years: camp out at the recreation department's offices the night before sign-ups."

That, Brams adds, was when her entire family agreed to consider moving to a smaller town with a slower pace of life. Having an older brother living in Charleston, South Carolina, she decided to put out some feelers regarding job opportunities there. "I wanted to take my time, make several visits to the area, and go on numerous interviews before making a decision," she says. "Not working was never an option, but the last thing I wanted to do was jump from the frying pan to the fire. My intent was to take the summer off to enjoy my kids, then find a position that was a good fit."

By the fall of 1997, Brams had moved her family to the South Carolina coast and landed a job working for an accounting firm. "It's perfect. I do mostly consulting work with health care clients, so there's a lot of flexibility in my new job. My son is playing soccer, and the whole family seems happier here. Granted, I'm now making half the salary I was getting in Atlanta, and that has required making some adjustments. But the cost of living is lower here. Plus—best of all—my new bosses not only recognize, but encourage, the idea that family comes first."

THE JOYS OF TELECOMMUTING

Three years ago, Allison Holt Brummelkamp was putting in twelve- to fourteen-hour days as a vice president in the Los Angeles offices of public relations giant Golin/Harris Communications. With two small children at home, plus about an hour's commute each way to work through downtown L.A., her schedule was taking its toll. "I was extremely stressed out and quite miserable," she says. "I wanted a challenging job, but one with a less frantic schedule—plus I missed having some quality time with my kids."

To restore her sanity, Brummelkamp made a successful bid to her supervisor both for more flexible hours and telecommuting privileges. "I was the first in our company to propose such a deal, and I had to give up my vice presidency," she reports. "But, in turn, I was able to cut back to working four six-hour days a week at home, with one day spent at the office for meetings, picking up mail, and putting in face time."

The 20 percent pay cut Brummelkamp endured was well worth it, she adds. "And actually, I put in more like eight hours a day at home. Nevertheless, I'm able to be there to kiss my kids good-bye in the morning when they leave for school, and greet them at the door when they return in the afternoon. I can also help with homework and shuttle them to soccer practice and music lessons. This flexibility has made all the difference in the world in terms of my happiness and productivity levels. And while it took a good year for everyone to adjust to my new schedule, my boss is happy with my work." In fact, he keeps asking Brummelkamp when she's coming back to the office full-time, often dangling the possibility of a promotion to entice her. "But, for now, I'm perfectly content with the way things are," she says.

Amy Watson knows the feeling. As a mother of four—ages fourteen, eleven, nine, and seven—Watson's life is a constant juggling act. What helps her manage both her brood and her job as a manager for Western Bell is being able to work from home two days a week. "I honestly don't know how I managed to do it all before," she says. "This arrangement has made a huge difference in my life—and my overall attitude towards my job. For starters, it enables me to avoid a thirty-five-mile commute twice a week. More importantly, it means I can volunteer more often at my kids' schools. Or, I can go to my sons' baseball games and my daughter's soccer games in the afternoon without feeling guilty, then work in my home office at night from eight to ten."

Thanks to PCs, modems, fax machines, on-line services, and sophisticated phone messaging systems, some 9.2 million Americans (60 percent of whom are women) now work from their homes rather than offices at least part of the week. And that number is rising at a steady clip. Find/SVP, a technology research firm based in New York City, predicts that fourteen million employees—or 10 percent of the workforce—will be telecommuting by 2000.

For moms, the benefits of working at home are obvious: greater flexibility with their time and more interaction with their kids. But telecommuters report other perks as well—like less time and money spent on commuting, plus fewer hours wasted chitchatting at the water cooler and going to long, drawn-out meetings they don't really need to attend. Moreover, women who telecommute say they've definitely noticed a surge in productivity levels on days they work at home.

Companies who have begun offering telecommuting as an option to their employees have noticed increased productivity as well. At the Aetna Health Plans office in Richmond, Virginia, for example, supervisor Karen Stanford oversees fifteen claims processors who telecommute. "Productivity has increased by 29 percent in the two years these staffers have been working from home," she reports. "What's more, workers are making fewer mistakes, morale is up, and the company is saving at least $12,000 a year in office space."

MINDING THEIR OWN BUSINESSES

When her son, Brendan, was eighteen months old, Victoria Marina had a well-paying job working nights as a violinist in a theater orchestra in San Francisco. It might have been ideal, had her husband not also had a night job working as a saxophonist. "Something had to give," she felt.

"One night, I was sitting in the orchestra pit looking out at all those yuppie parents—and it hit me that there might be a market for music and dance classes geared to very young children," Marina speculated. The following spring, she launched Tunes for Tots, running an advertisement in the local newspaper and offering classes in her home. With no competition in the area, the response was overwhelming. Four months later, Marina was forced to lease studio space—and hire two additional teachers—to accommodate her students.

As a toddler, son Brendan was among her pupils. And, as he grew older, she was able to work her classes around his school hours. "I loved the creative outlet the job offered, but most of all, I treasured the time it allowed me to spend with my child," she says.

These days, Tunes for Tots is still going strong, but Marina's career has switched gears again. "I still run the school, but I no longer teach." Instead, she uses her musical expertise to do a combination of personal counseling and healing work. "Women make up the bulk of my clientele," she explains. "I lead a women's circle that meets twice a month which incorporates music, rhythm, and singing as a form of therapy. I also work one-on-one with clients to help them discover who they are, which often entails finding ways to let go of who they aren't. It's work that I find not only challenging, but personally fulfilling." From this work, Marina, who's now a single mom, has also developed a music CD that has been distributed worldwide.

In fact, just like Tunes for Tots, Marina's latest ventures have been lucrative as well. "I'm living proof of the adage 'Do what you love, and the money will follow,'" she adds.

Susan Lammers agrees. In 1993, this mother of two young children was putting in twelve-hour days at Microsoft. "No one else there had kids, and I didn't feel comfortable leaving to pick up my son from preschool or to take my kids to the doctor," she says. "In fact, I felt constrained by the whole system. They wanted work and family separated, but I wanted them integrated—like the family farm of the agricultural age."

Lammers got her wish when she decided to quit the software giant and start an educational software company of her own, Headbone Interactive. "I chose a location just five minutes from my son's school so I wouldn't miss things like the Thanksgiving party or the school play," she reports. She also chose to offer her employees flexible hours as well as permission to bring their kids to work. "I put a giant toy box just outside my office for all the kids to enjoy," she adds. These days, Lammers's seven-year-old son is a frequent visitor at Headbone. "He tests all of our software and has earned the nickname 'Captain Research,'" she says.

To date, Headbone has released eight popular educational CD-ROM titles and boasts revenues of about $2 million per year.

In their quest for success, staggering numbers of women have launched their own businesses. Even as the rest of corporate America has tightened its belt, women-owned companies continue to be fruitful and multiply. In fact, studies show that the number of women-owned businesses has jumped 42 percent over the last three years, and collectively, they now hire more workers in the United States than the Fortune 500 companies do globally. Figuratively speaking, eight million women-owned firms in the United States today generate more than $2.3 trillion in annual sales.

What are the most common reasons women cite for venturing out on their own? Control of their futures, their financial destinies, and—above all—their time.

AT LAST ... WE'RE IN THE MONEY!

The good news is that financing for women-owned businesses has never been more plentiful. After decades of being snubbed by banks that considered them bad credit risks, female entrepreneurs have become a hot commodity. Indeed, these days, women business owners are often on the *receiving* end of letters and telephone calls from loan officers.

Some major milestones: in 1995, Wells Fargo Bank and the National Association of Women Business Owners established the first nationwide private loan fund (totaling $1 billion) specifically targeted to women business owners.

In 1997, working with Women Incorporated, Bank of America launched a similar program. "We are seeing an explosion of female entrepreneurship, and we are eager to meet the needs of business owners," says Bank of America executive vice president Kathleen Brown. "Last year, Bank of America committed to lend $10.6 billion to small businesses over three years, and we expect that about thirty to forty percent of that will finance women-owned businesses, based on the makeup of the small business segment. But there is no upper limit. Women are starting businesses at twice the rate of men and are expected to own 50 percent of all small businesses by the year 2000."

Chase Manhattan Bank has set up a toll-free lending hotline for women business owners in New York and New Jersey. Barnett Bank, based in Jacksonville, Florida, has pledged to lend $500 million to women-owned companies in Florida and Georgia in a joint program with the National Association of Women Business Owners of Florida. A slew of regional lenders has also begun freeing up funds for female entrepreneurs (see Resources).

"Bankers are just starting to realize the power of women-owned businesses in the economy," confirms Ronald Wesson, vice president of Dun and Bradstreet's new Minority and Women-Owned Business Development Group, which recently began to market an expanded version of what it calls "the world's largest database of women-owned firms."

THERE'S NO PLACE LIKE HOME

A whopping 3.6 million women-owned businesses today are home-based—and with good reason. "More and more women are choosing to abandon the nine-to-five grind in favor of options that offer more freedom, flexibility, and time with their families," notes Priscilla Huff, author of *101 Best Home-Based Businesses for Women*. Recent studies reveal that the majority of women who run their own small businesses aren't making a killing—overall, they earn only 35 percent of what men who run their own small businesses earn. But on the flip side, a quarter of these women are earning between $100,000 and $499,000 per year in their ventures, and nine percent boast incomes of $500,000 and up.

More important than money, however, is the freedom and flexibility that owning a small business offers. Thus, it's not surprising that the number of women in these ranks is growing dramatically. Indeed, according to a new work-at-home survey conducted by Link Resources, a New York City–based market research consulting firm, women are starting their own home-based businesses at the astonishing rate of one every thirty-five seconds!

Rebecca Bostick is among that number. Eight years ago, the architectural firm she worked for in Alexandria, Virginia, decided to relocate. "To stay with the company would have meant a commute of thirty-five to fifty-five minutes on a good day," she says. "With a newborn at home, I knew there had to be a better way to run my life."

Having already completed some independent projects on the side, Bostick figured she'd give working at home on her own a shot. Today, Bostick is a mother of three, and her business is still going strong—grossing about $100,000 a year. "Even better than the money, I love the flexible hours and the opportunity they give me to balance work and family," she says.

Diane Ennen of Pompano Beach, Florida, doesn't make nearly the salary Bostick does, but she's equally content running Ennen Computer Services (ECS) from the comfort of her home office. She launched the business soon after having her first child. Working as a secretary in corporate America at the time, Ennen had every intention of putting her son in day care. "But that lasted only two weeks," she says. "It was too hard for me to let him go. Plus, having worked in my field for over ten years, I felt I had the skills to do just as well working at home."

The bulk of Ennen's business comes from area doctors and lawyers who need medical and legal transcripts typed. She also types résumés, handles correspondence for new businesses, and tutors clients on how to use various kinds of computer software.

Ennen's oldest is now twelve. She also has a three-year-old daughter and a baby on the way. "I often get up early to put in two to three good hours of work before my kids wake up," she says. Sometimes she manages to get in an hour or two mid-afternoon while her kids nap or play nearby. "My home looks like the set of *Romper Room*," she admits. "But I don't have trouble staying focused."

Occasionally, Ennen puts in another hour or so at night after tucking her kids into bed. "This is probably not a typical work-at-home mom's schedule, but I prefer it this way, because I get to spend a lot of quality time during the day with my kids," she adds. "And that is my *favorite* job!"

WHEN TWO HEADS ARE BETTER THAN ONE

Yet another way for moms to keep a foot in the door at work while raising a family is to find someone else who wants to do the same, then split the job 50-50. According to a new survey by Watson Wyatt Worldwide, job sharing is growing in popularity. Currently, 50 percent of large companies polled—and 31 percent of all respondents—embrace the concept.

Patty Konwinski was an employment representative at Steelcase, the Grand Rapids, Michigan–based office furniture company, when her first child was born in 1985. "I was going crazy trying to juggle both jobs," she recalls. "Life was a blur. I had no time for my son, my husband, or myself. It was awful."

Watching from the sidelines was colleague Marti O'Brien, who soon learned she was pregnant. "When Marti approached me and suggested we share a job, it was the perfect solution," Konwinski says. "The tug-of-war between work and family was really getting to me, but having worked since I was twelve, I couldn't imagine myself as a full-time mom and homemaker."

The two put their heads and talents together to come up with a proposal to persuade management to go for their idea. "At the time, Steelcase allowed job sharing, but not at the professional level," according to Konwinski. As luck would have it, the manager they had to win over was a mom herself who had worked when her children were young. She was receptive to the idea, and the job sharers were given a trial period to prove that their arrangement could work.

For eight years, both Konwinski and O'Brien blossomed under their 50-50 partnership. Each worked two and a half days per week and received half the salary and benefits they did while working full-time. To keep things running smoothly, the two met for lunch on a weekly basis to discuss upcoming events and projects.

In fact, the partnership turned out to be a win-win situation all around. Earning kudos for their work from both clients and management, the two were promoted in 1989 to senior employment representatives. Three years later, they applied for—and landed—another position up the ladder, this time in marketing.

In 1993, following the birth of her second child, O'Brien decided to quit her half of the job to stay at home with her little ones full-time. "Almost immediately, I was approached by another woman in the company who wanted to let me share her job," Konwinski asserts. Vera Allen, a full-time program manager at Steelcase, was a grandmother seeking flexible hours so she could start her own business on the side. "Once again, we had to sell our plan to her boss," says Konwinski, who by then was a mother of three boys. "When we succeeded, it was the first time job sharing was allowed in a management position at Steelcase."

That partnership thrived for nearly two years, until Allen also decided to leave the company. "I had lots of people approach me to fill Vera's shoes," says Konwinski. "But, instead, I decided to post the position and interview women. I knew to keep things running smoothly, I had to find just the right person."

That person turned out to be Diane Liggins, a mother of two small children, and the pair's working relationship has been a perfect fit. "I now work school hours (eight-forty-five to two-forty-five) four days a week, and Diane works two and a half days, so there's some overlap," Konwinski reports.

"Being able to job-share has saved my sanity," she adds. "My boys are now seven, nine, and twelve, and I like being able to pick them up from school and spend the afternoon with them. On my off days, I do a lot of volunteer work at their schools. Growing up, I remember seeing my mom at my school frequently, and that al-

121

ways meant a lot to me. Now I'm doing the same for my kids, and I'm convinced that doing so sends them the message that school is important."

Of course, a job-sharing partner doesn't have to be another working mother—nor even a woman for that matter. Until recently, Peggy and David Andrews of Minneapolis shared a marriage, a child, *and* a job as a leadership development consultant at American Express Financial Advisors in the Twin Cities.

"When our daughter was born in May of 1996, both of us wanted to be actively involved parents," Peggy notes. "Yet, neither of us wanted to give up our careers." The Andrewses spent four months pitching their arrangement to American Express. "We promised to take responsibility for communicating with each other and our team members. We also agreed to cover for each other in case of an illness, to maintain a daily computer log of projects and meetings, and to function as a mini self-managed work team," Peggy adds.

The couple worked out a rotating shift. One week, David would go to the office three days, while Peggy stayed at home with their daughter; then David would be at home for two days while Peggy went to work. The next week, they reversed their days at home and work. In between, they kept in touch by e-mail, voice mail, and nightly briefings at home. Both agree that job sharing made them better at all they did. "It was more than balance, it was synergy," Peggy says. "My work enhanced my performance in the family and vice versa. I was a peak performer at home and at work."

Kathi Tunheim, director of leadership development at American Express, agrees. "I got the best of both styles. Peggy's work was really creative. She had lots of ideas, and she was very expressive. Then I got David's attention to detail and analytical viewpoint."

In addition to sharing one office, one computer, and the benefits of one employee, the Andrewses also managed to get by on one paycheck. But both felt the financial sacrifice was worth it. "Not only did we have more time to spend with our daughter, we had more free time than most working parents," Peggy says. "I was able to start on my master's degree in human development, and David refinished furniture and took an architectural drawing class."

Last year, the couple also launched a small consulting company on the side, HR2000. Besides, heading up work-family seminars entitled "Creating a Life That Works for You," the Andrewses recently decided to give up their American Express job to devote more time to their business. "We're still job sharing," Peggy says. "The only difference is, now *we* own the company."

Adds David of his evolving partnership with his wife, "I look at it as a new paradigm or strategy. Previously, the only options for parents have been full-time day care or one parent home full-time. We simply said, 'Let's take a husband and wife. How could they share work and family so they each have involvement in both, and increase their joy and peace?'"

HOW PUTTING FAMILY FIRST AFFECTS YOUR PAYCHECK

Naturally, choosing to work fewer hours—by way of switching to part-time work or job sharing—means making less money. Mothers who take lengthy maternity leaves also appear to suffer financially. To what extent?

As much as 33 percent loss of income the first year and up to 20 percent three to five years later, when they return to work, according to one study.

But what about mothers who find ways—for example, via flexible hours or telecommuting—to balance full-time work with raising their families? Financially speaking, it would seem logical that people who make their careers top priority would be more successful at work. But according to a new University of Pennsylvania study, this is not necessarily the rule. The study, which tracked the earning power of more than twenty-two hundred women and men for fourteen years after high school, discovered that those who had marked family life "very important" on their initial questionnaires earned about 7 percent more than those who'd answered "not important." The study's authors believe that "the 'family-first' group were more settled in their private lives and could focus more on their careers."

BEING A MOM IS "THE BESTEST"

But as most any mother—regardless of her work schedule—will tell you, it's not just about money. No paycheck can even come close to matching the joyful experiences associated with parenthood.

Gina Barrett Schlesinger, president of Speaker Services, Inc., a Springfield, Pennsylvania–based professional speakers bureau, agrees. "When my youngest daughter, Gillian, was four, I remember being in a huge hurry one night," recalls the thirty-eight-year-old mother of two. "I was rushing through our dining room dressed in my best suit and entirely focused on getting ready for an evening meeting, when I found Gillian dancing about to one of her favorite oldies, 'Cool,' from *West Side Story*. I knew I was running late, and yet, I couldn't resist reaching out to grab her hand and spinning her around. My then seven-year-old daughter Caitlin quickly came into our orbit, and I grabbed her, too. The three of us did a wild jitterbug around the dining room and into the living room. We were having a blast."

When the song ended, Schlesinger patted the girls' bottoms and sent them upstairs for their baths. "I went back to business and was bent over shoving papers into my briefcase when I overheard my youngest say to her sister, 'Caitlin, isn't Mommy the bestest one?'"

"How close I had come to missing that moment," she recalls. "I remember my mind drifting immediately to the awards and diplomas that covered the walls of my office, and I decided then and there that no award, no achievement I had ever earned could match what I'd just experienced."

Five years later, Schlesinger still treasures that special moment. "I don't expect my child to utter such a phrase at age fourteen," she says. "But at age forty, if she bends down over that pine box to say good-bye to the cast-off container of my soul, I want her to say it then.

" *'Isn't Mommy the bestest one?'* It doesn't fit on my résumé. But I want it on my tombstone."

CHAPTER TEN

Passion with a Purpose:
Doing Well by Doing Good

I began to have an idea of my life, not as the slow shaping of achievement to fit my preconceived purposes, but as the gradual discovery and growth of a purpose which I did not know.

—JOANNA FIELD

In the summer of 1994, as she was celebrating her fortieth birthday, America's reigning talk-show queen, Oprah Winfrey, had an opportunity to watch her competitors' shows. She didn't particularly like what she saw and decided to take a second look at her own show and the message it was sending.

Ultimately, Winfrey opted to reject the scandal route by turning her show toward more positive topics. It was a risky move—and, in fact, ratings initially tumbled a bit. But Winfrey didn't care. "I feel really good about the changes," she says. "I have a new peace of mind. And I never worry about falling from the top. I'm always trying to figure out how to take the power I have and use it."

That power is undeniable. By introducing a monthly on-air book club two years ago, for example, Winfrey has single-handedly gotten Americans reading again, and every book she has featured has become a best-seller. Moreover, in 1997, she introduced a new charity project called "Oprah's Angels Network" that has stirred a frenzy of generosity nationwide. Initially, she challenged corporations to join her in helping Habitat for Humanity build a house in every market where her show is seen. Then she invited viewers to collect change in their communities. According to Winfrey, the money raised will be used to send at least fifty kids to college.

Oprah's ever-growing list of other charitable causes is endless. She has funded scholarships at both her alma mater—Tennessee State University—and at Morehouse College. She has donated $500,000 to keep the Chicago Academy for the Arts high school open and a whopping $1 million to an inner-city Chicago high school. Always a staunch advocate of children's rights—indeed, Winfrey once tearfully confessed on the air that she was abused as a child—she has served as a vocal spokesperson against child abuse. In fact, a bill Winfrey proposed to Congress calling for the establishment of a national database of all convicted child abusers was signed into law by President Clinton in December of 1993.

ALTRUISM IS ALIVE AND WELL

Incorporating a sense of ethics and values at work is of paramount importance to many women today who no longer believe in measuring success solely in terms of status, wealth, and personal accomplishment. Paychecks and profits still matter, of course, but no longer are they sufficient to sustain a feeling of true success.

In fact, everywhere we turned, we found successful women looking beyond themselves to help others succeed. Some were big names you'll recognize; others were everyday women who are redefining success by contributing selflessly to a greater good. Regardless, their work-life success stories will inspire you.

PIONEERS OF CORPORATE SOCIAL RESPONSIBILITY

Gun Denhart, founder and CEO of Hanna Andersson, a mail-order children's clothing company based in Portland, Oregon, began practicing socially responsible business long before it was trendy. "There's more to measuring success than profit statements," she has always believed.

Since 1983, when she first established her business, one of Denhart's top priorities was to create "a company with heart." To meet that goal, she quickly launched what's called the Hannadowns program. Through Hannadowns, customers are encouraged to return outgrown "hannas"—Swedish-style togs of legendary durability— for a 20 percent credit on future purchases. The steady stream of garments the company receives goes to needy children from flood-stricken areas in the United States and to orphanages in Romania and Kazakhstan. To date, the company has passed on close to a million pieces of clothing. "Hannadowns very much defines who we are as a company," says Denhart, whose firm also donates 5 percent of its profits each year to charities hand-picked by its workers.

In September 1997, the company also launched its "Cash for Kids" program, in which 123 Portland school children received a $100 check to take directly to their classrooms to help purchase workbooks, computer software, and geology kits. Twelve other Portland companies participated in this first annual event, and Hanna Andersson's goal is to double that number by 1998.

Another successful business with heart is The Body Shop International. Founder and CEO Anita Roddick has a plaque above her office that reads "Department of the Future." "In the future, I don't see how business can operate in isolation of the community," she explains. "And one of the most important jobs I have is to develop more opportunities for our staff to spend company time in the service of the local community. I believe that people are able to measure their greatness by these experiences and find the heroes in themselves by caring for others."

Already, all employees of The Body Shop are allowed paid time off—half a day per month—to take part in a community project of their choice. "Whether caring for locally disadvantaged people, cleaning up the local environment, or working with sick animals, staff can feel connected and uplifted," Roddick believes.

Laura Scher, cofounder of Working Assets Long Distance, a competitor of Sprint and MCI, is also devoted to a double bottom line. In 1993, the San Francisco–based company invited customers to make donations to aid war victims in Bosnia by rounding up payments on their monthly bills. Working Assets subsequently donated $50,000 to Bosnian relief organizations.

Since then, Working Assets has been using its two

products—in addition to long-distance services, the company offers a credit card with similar benefits—to raise funds for a host of liberal social and economic causes. The company itself also donates 1 percent of the price of every call made. To date, recipient organizations, which are chosen by the company's customers themselves, have included Greenpeace, Planned Parenthood, and the Gay and Lesbian Alliance Against Defamation. But it's not just the big guns who are finding ways to positively impact and help society.

"I SHOULD HAVE BEEN A STATISTIC"

Whenever Demetrus Alexander sees the title that follows her name on the company letterhead she uses, the thirty-eight-year-old vice president of Warner Alliance Records can't help but pinch herself. "I grew up in the housing projects of Nashville, Tennessee, and for the first half of my life, it looked as though I'd never get out," she recalls.

In fact, by age sixteen, Alexander was an unwed mother. A second child followed when she was twenty-one. "But I always wanted something better—for me and for other young single mothers," she says. Ultimately, it was her strong, clear voice and love for gospel music that got her out of the ghetto. "I began organizing neighborhood concerts and choir performances at my church to raise funds for local community service programs. The intent was to use the money to help youngsters get jobs and stay out of trouble," she reports. Along the way, Alexander landed a job herself, working as a receptionist for Warner Alliance Records, the gospel division of the Time Warner music empire.

Despite her amazing climb to a vice presidency, Alexander hasn't forgotten her roots, nor her commitment to help others still stuck in the projects. In addition to volunteering and raising money for groups such as the Bethlehem Centers of Nashville, which provides tutoring, sports clinics, day care, and other services for low-income families, Alexander is active in several national organizations. She is a founding member of The United Gospel Industry Council, a coalition of gospel recording artists and executives who develop community programs. In 1995, she also cofounded—with gospel singer CeCe Winans—My Sister's Keeper, an organization that provides counseling for troubled women, particularly unwed teenage mothers. "I should have been a statistic," she says. "And yet, I beat the odds. Now it's important to me to make sure that others do the same."

TLC FOR AIDS VICTIMS

Kathleen Dodd is founder and president of The Corridor Group, Inc., a proprietary health care consulting organization headquartered in Overland, Kansas. In 1995, she founded Katy's Place, a nonprofit organization designed to serve the needs of women and children affected by the AIDS virus. "Its beginnings were born out of my love for children and my desire to become involved in the community," Dodd says.

Children whose lives have been touched by tragedy ring close to home for Dodd, who lost her own mother when she was only ten. "I was left with many indelible memories that, in part, define who I am today," she says. With both a personal and professional interest in educating the growing needs of women and children. Dodd's decision to focus on AIDS came about when she learned that the deadly virus was rising fastest among these two constituencies. Yet, in most communities—including her own—very few resources were available to meet the special needs of this population.

"I believe that the solution to this dilemma lies in a proactive approach," says Dodd. "Yet, my attempts at being proactive in this endeavor have been fraught with obstacles, including a social stigma associated with the disease, a lack of recognition for a family's basic needs, service fragmentation, a lack of focus on the specific issues of women and children affected by AIDS, and an obvious shortfall in monetary and program resources geared to this very specific population."

Fortunately, Katy's Place is making progress in dealing with many of these obstacles. Katy's Closet provides sundries and clothing items to those in need of basic necessities. "The future focus of our organization is to provide case management and a respite facility for children whose parents are not able to provide care for them," says Dodd.

Progress in educating others, however—from unaffected women and teens, to legislators and community leaders—has been painstakingly slow. "Working through the various layers of bureaucracy can be time-consuming and complex," Dodd laments.

In fact, many have told Dodd that her pet project won't succeed. But she refuses to lose sight of her goal. "Being philanthropic is not something that can be taught or acquired," she believes. "It's an obligation that comes from within your soul and pushes you to accept the mantle of responsibility. The passion and effort I bring to this endeavor is what distinguishes me and makes me unique. I have all the confidence that our efforts will be rewarded and that the deserving will share in the generosity of the good people who have been so supportive of Katy's Place."

HIRING FROM THE "HOOD" TO SERVE THE "HOOD"

Gwen Johnson put in twenty-five years as a business teacher and guidance counselor for the Cleveland, Ohio, school system. But when her elderly mother became ill and needed a part-time nurse, Johnson stumbled upon a business opportunity. "Many of the home health care agencies I contacted were wary of traveling to black city neighborhoods," she explains. Thus, in 1992, Gwen and her son, Eric, combined their names and established Geric Home Health Care.

"As unknowns in the business, customers were initially wary of us," Gwen reports. "So we approached nursing homes, hospitals, and public agencies with an irresistible pitch: 'Give us the cases nobody else will take.'" Their strategy worked, and today, Geric Home Health Care boasts annual sales of $12 million and has expanded its service area to include Detroit and Gary, Indiana, as well as Cleveland.

Financial success is nice, mother and son agree, but equally uplifting is seeing the results of the services they are providing—and not solely to their patients. "We mostly hire single welfare mothers to do the work. In essence, we put neighbors to work helping neighbors," says Gwen. Or, as Eric puts it, "We hire from the 'hood' to serve the 'hood.'"

Mobilizing this workforce has required a tremendous

amount of effort. "We set up a state-certified school for nursing aides and hired an educational director," Gwen reports. Recognizing that they would have a lot of unwed teenage mothers as applicants, Geric also concentrated the school's curriculum into a month of daytime classes, a schedule that would enable moms to attend while their kids were in school.

Once students become employees, their casework is scheduled around child-care constraints and clustered by bus route.

Nursing aides at Geric who want to advance their careers can enroll in LPN or RN training and receive half their tuition from the company. "We can then sell their services at a higher rate or put them to work in management," Gwen says.

In a business known for its high turnover rate, Geric's, not surprisingly, runs less than 25 percent a year.

ONE WOMAN'S LOSS IS AN ENTIRE COMMUNITY'S GAIN

Seventeen years ago, at the age of thirty-seven, Susan Zimmerman's husband suffered a fatal heart attack. "This followed an eight-year battle with testicular cancer, which he had survived and been pronounced cured," she says. Her husband's death left Zimmerman with two small children to support. Just thirty-four at the time, she was working in a low-level secretarial job with a salary she knew wouldn't sustain her family. To rebuild their lives, Zimmerman went back to school, earning a bachelor's degree in communications and a master's in labor relations. She then found a job in the president's office of her alma mater, Michigan State University.

That she was able to land on her feet after such a tragic loss was an amazing accomplishment in itself. But Zimmerman, despite her grief, managed to summon the time, energy, and devotion to make a difference in her community as well. Unable to find a support group to turn to after losing her husband, she decided to establish a bereavement group of her own. To date, under the auspices of The Widowed Person's Group, Zimmerman has touched the lives of nearly five hundred individuals in the East Lansing area, including many young widows whom she has inspired to follow in her footsteps by undertaking a college program to rebuild their lives.

In 1990, Zimmerman, now a fifty-one-year-old program director for the Michigan State University Alumni Association, also founded Integra, an international non-profit organization. "Integra provides a vast array of resources and programs that offer support in dealing with all kinds of losses," she explains. "We have both an international board of directors and a local board. Our three missions are to provide education and training— primarily to doctors, nurses, and others in health care— to fund research in the area of grief and loss, and to provide outreach services to people in need all over the world."

Integra is innovative in that it incorporates the arts in many of its outreach programs. "Recently, we sponsored a series of concerts featuring a Danish jazz musician who specializes in playing impromptu musical responses to individuals' personal stories of loss. It's difficult to describe in words, but those who have participated in these healing workshops have reported feeling deeply moved by the experience. In fact, they often claim, 'The music was inside of me—he just pulled it out.'"

In the area of research, Integra is also on the cutting

edge. "We have developed a test—much like the Myers-Briggs Inventory psychologists use—that allows professionals to pinpoint exactly where someone is in the grieving process," Zimmerman adds. "And this can be extremely beneficial when providing assistance and therapy."

SHARING THE WEALTH AND LEADING BY EXAMPLE

Muriel Siebert has always been a pioneer of sorts. Three decades ago, she made historic waves when she applied to become the first female member of the New York Stock Exchange. Although she had risen to a partnership in a leading Wall Street brokerage firm and had made big money for colleagues, her effort was patronized, ridiculed, or openly opposed by many men on Wall Street. In fact, she was turned down by nine of the first ten men she asked to sponsor her application.

Today, at sixty-four, she is CEO of her own discount brokerage firm, Muriel Siebert & Company, and continues to speak up and speak out for women and minorities in business. "The men at the top of industry and government should be more willing to risk sharing leadership with women and minority members who are not merely clones of their white male buddies," she insists. "In these fast-changing times, we need the different viewpoints and experiences, and we need the enlarged talent bank. The real risk lies in continuing to do things the way they've always been done."

Always one to speak her mind, Siebert says one of her biggest beefs these days is the sense of greed she sees permeating Wall Street and the financial community.

Association's top honor for her outstanding accomplishments and services as a mentor to female entrepreneurs.

"Being a woman never really held me back, but I know that's not the case for others," says Moddelmug, who currently mentors two area entrepreneurs. "We still have to be concerned about women having the opportunity to move ahead in business. That's why I try to help others achieve their potential."

LINKING WOMEN TO POWER

Sixteen years ago, Barb Moore finished her MBA and bought into the family business, Anderson Transfer, Inc., a moving company based in Washington, Pennsylvania. She'd always been content with her career, but after nine years in the business, Moore got fed up with the fact that she'd never met another woman with a business larger than hers. "I was frustrated with the lack of mentors and role models—especially working in a male-oriented business," she says. "There was no one like me to turn to for advice, or just to compare notes with."

Thus, in 1990, Moore and a colleague founded PowerLink, Inc. "After asking ourselves, 'Why are there no women out there with $10 to $20 million companies?' we concluded that men had a decisive edge because they were doing all the networking on that level," Moore explains. "After all, at the time, men comprised the majority of business-school graduates, so they were the ones making lifetime career contacts. Women, on the other hand, were certainly running their fair share of businesses, but these tended to be very small. And we believed the reason for that was because women—who prefer to work with other women—had nowhere to go to get help growing their businesses."

PowerLink has since helped to change all that by providing advisory boards for women-owned firms. "These boards are made up of volunteers who work with a business for one year, providing much-needed expertise these women couldn't otherwise afford," Moore explains. Services offered by these boards run the gamut from troubleshooting and problem-solving, to implementing strategies to expand the size of these women-owned businesses.

Thus far, PowerLink has orchestrated advisory boards for forty-three women-owned companies and boasts many success stories. "For example, one woman we worked with had a somewhat successful telemarketing contract company, but her average sale per customer was only $300," according to Moore. "The advisory board we put together for her told her she was wasting her time going after small accounts. They persuaded her to take out a loan and expand her business. They also coached her on how to hire better employees. Today that woman doesn't even bid on jobs under $10,000."

HELPING THE NEXT GENERATION SCORE

Weekdays, Stephanie Streeter puts in long hours as a group vice president at Avery Dennison, a maker of adhesives and labels based in Pasadena, California. Her office products division brings in nearly a third of Avery's $3.2 billion in revenue. But on most weekends, Streeter can be found with her husband in a gymnasium on Los

Angeles's west side teaching preteen girls how to play basketball. "Actually, it may *look* like basketball to you," she says, "but I believe we're helping to train the next generation of female executives."

How so? "Most boys learn team sports as a matter of course and apply the lessons they learn to the grown-up business world," she explains. "But most girls suffer because they don't. That's why I'm always telling their moms and dads that team-playing will be an important asset to them down the line."

Streeter should know, having grown up in Los Angeles and played varsity basketball at Stanford University for four years. Now thirty-nine, the five-foot-eight-inch former power forward and guard says that so much of what has made her successful in business today she learned on the basketball court. "Basketball teaches you when you need to lead and when not to. Only one person can have the ball at a time," she says. "You also learn what it feels like to miss a free throw at the end of the game and how to deal with it. You can walk away from it at the end, then replay what you did to see what went wrong." Mastering skills like these, she believes, can make you a high scorer both on the court and in your career.

DOING WHAT SHE LOVES AND LOVING WHAT SHE'S DOING

Rebecca Maddox's résumé sparkles. Over a sixteen-year period in corporate America, she has worked for blue-chip corporations such as Revlon, Arthur Andersen, Citicorp, and CompuCard. She has held important titles as well—including vice president, senior vice president, and divisional president. "I was the model executive—committed and self-motivated, working nights and weekends, sweating the details," she says. "I met every deadline, obsessed as I was with getting through my in-box, and doing well. Each company I worked for received more than a fair return for every dollar it paid me."

In fact, Maddox has made big bucks throughout her career—"more than I ever dreamed possible," she admits. She's had clout, too. "I had large staffs, controlled hefty yearly budgets, presented strategies to boards of directors, participated in high-level policy decisions. For most of my career, I also had profit-and-loss accountability, that often nerve-wracking but much sought-after sign of *real* power in the corporation."

Then in 1990, while working as a senior vice president for a division of a diversified financial services company worth nearly $20 billion, Maddox was asked to head up a new project. "The CEO asked me to establish an 'intrapreneurial' entity—an independent company within the company," she reports. "The goal was to create a new business and a new way of doing business."

Leery at first, Maddox eventually couldn't resist the challenge after hearing what her boss had in mind. "He gave me two parameters regarding what I needed to accomplish," she says. "First, I had to design and create a company that could produce sales of at least $500 million a year. Second, the business had to be relationship-based."

In fact, what Maddox's boss had in mind was a company that would relate to individual customers the way Jimmy Stewart's George Bailey related to his in *It's a Wonderful Life*. "We were going to do business with people on the basis of knowing them well and put our trust in the strength of their character as much as in the strength of their balance sheet," Maddox explains. "And it was entirely up to me to identify a market, develop a plan for the service we would bring to that market, and sell the idea to our board of directors."

Facing this monumental task, Maddox knew one thing immediately: she wanted to work with women. "Their executive power was still invisible to corporate America," she explains. "No company was doing a particularly good job of communicating with women and offering legitimate solutions to meet their real needs." She then decided to narrow her focus from women to female entrepreneurs. "After doing a lot of research, I discovered that not only was this a largely ignored market group, but these women were actually succeeding at a higher rate than their male counterparts," she says.

From day one, public reaction to Maddox's venture was phenomenal. "We sent out press releases, but never spent a dime on advertising," she reveals. "Our business was fueled entirely by word-of-mouth and media interest. We were widely hailed as the first for-profit corporation that was prepared to address the needs of the women business owners market, including making capital available to them."

But by April of 1993, Maddox began hearing grumblings from senior management, who were beginning to think that maybe this new venture wasn't such a good fit—strategically speaking—with the parent company's other operations. "I knew we were in trouble," Maddox recalls. And sure enough, the rug was soon pulled out from under them.

"I was destroyed inside," Maddox admits. "I can't really express what was torn out of me. They'd taken something that I cared deeply about. I loved what I was doing in a way that I had never known before."

Contemplating her next move, Maddox wondered, "Should I find another corporate job?" But she couldn't get comfortable with that option. "These women had become much more than statistics, much more than a market to me," she says. "They'd become real people, real faces, real lives to me. And they were suddenly back where they'd started—with no one to meet their needs in the way that we'd been prepared to do." Ultimately, Maddox made the decision to "divorce" the corporation she'd been affiliated with and become a female entrepreneur herself. As a result, a new company, Capital Rose, Inc., was born.

"Capital Rose is not a cause," she says. "We are problem-solvers. We have created the Capital Rose Perpetual Fund, a not-for-profit corporation, and set a goal of raising $40 million to finance women-owned businesses. We're doing this by asking four million men and women to contribute $10 each. It's a national effort. It's grass-roots."

Capital Rose is also on a crusade of sorts, sharing its knowledge and experience about the women's market with corporations throughout the nation—and in all industries, from manufacturing and financial services to consumer marketing and professional service firms. "We believe that if we assist corporations in providing products and services that truly meet the real needs of women—and women business owners—we are fulfilling our mission," Maddox says. "In short, we are helping to make women business owners real, visible, and economically important to corporations."

Doing what she loves—and loving what she's doing—keeps Maddox, who's shared her expertise in a book entitled *Inc. Your Dreams,* extremely motivated. "We're building legacies for our families, our colleagues, our communities," she says. "We're acting on our right to self-reliance. We're seeking dignity.

"I believe that those are goals that all of us can reach, in any walk of life," she adds. "For some of us, business ownership is the choice for attaining them. For others, the answer lies elsewhere. What matters is that each of us finds her way, and that we all move forward together."

SECTION THREE

• • •

Finding Solutions for Work-Life Conflicts

CHAPTER ELEVEN

To Thine Own Self Be True: Rewriting Your Own Script

What is right for one soul may not be right for another. It may mean having to stand on your own and do something strange in the eyes of others.

—EILEEN CADDY

In chapter one we asked you to define success. Now we ask you to repeat the process. Throughout the previous chapters, you have heard the voices of a chorus of women who, in one way or another, had reached a crossroads in their lives that led them to redefine success. Perhaps you have decided by now to join their ranks.

SUCCESS IS NOT ONE-SIZE-FITS-ALL

There is, of course, no one path to success. Indeed, the women whose stories we've shared in this text have chosen their own paths, followed their own instincts, and made their own rules to redefine success on their own terms. Some, you'll recall, have shed their Wonder Woman costumes in search of more equilibrium in their lives. For identical reasons, others have stepped off the promotion path or decided to backtrack in their careers—at least temporarily. Many have traded in mundane, joyless jobs for careers that give them a greater sense of meaning and purpose. Others have decided that calling the shots themselves is what makes them happiest, and as a result, they are creating businesses with heart. Still others—especially moms—have found ways to juggle satisfying careers without losing family focus.

Along the way, all of these women have grappled with redefining success but found that by giving themselves permission to change the rules, their stories end in balance and joy. Your game plan will likely differ from theirs, but we hope you'll look to these women for support, validation, inspiration, and even solutions.

GOOD ADVICE

For help in rewriting your own script, here's what we recommend:

Be careful not to dismiss the importance of work

"Work is a precious commodity in a high-quality life," says Barbara L. Pagano, Ed.S. a Gulf Breeze, Florida–based executive development consultant. "We can choose lower but livable wages. We can survive on lateral versus hierarchical career moves. But it pays to seek work that we find interesting and challenging." Indeed, out of 744 factors in a recent Duke University study on longevity, the number-one factor associated with a long life was "work satisfaction."

Take the time to poll yourself

Rediscovering who you are and what you really want out of life is the key to true success. Throughout this book, we have shared dozens of survey results with you regarding what women crave most to achieve all-around happiness. These results may be enlightening—and even beneficial—to you, but to write your own script, we encourage you to take the time to poll yourself.

"When I ask a grown person—whether they're thirty or forty or fifty—'What do you really love to do?' what I often hear is, 'Gosh, I don't know,'" says Jacqueline McMakin, codirector of Working from the Heart, a career counseling center in McLean, Virginia. The problem is, people often choose their careers by exploring and responding to "what's out there," then wonder why they're unhappy. A better way? Take time to discover who you are, what you care about, what you like doing, and what you're good at.

Manhattan therapist and career counselor Barbara Sher, author of *I Could Do Anything If I Only Knew What It Was* and *Live the Life You Love,* agrees. "What will really carry you where you want to go is your wishes, which reflect what you love. You'll never be happy and you'll never be brilliant at what you're doing unless you're doing what you love," she says. And to figure that out? Sher advises taking a set of ten three-by-five-inch index cards and noting one of your top career dreams or goals on each one. Then, flip through your "wish deck" and identify the one "heart-stopper," or single goal whose attainment you absolutely cherish the most.

Consider hiring a career "doctor"

Nothing jumps out at you, or your top career dream/ goal doesn't seem feasible? Career confusion is far more common than you think, especially among women in their thirties and forties. But it's never too late to get help. To find a professional who can help you sort things out, ask friends or colleagues for referrals. Or, call the National Board for Certified Counselors. (See the Resources section for this organization's and other helpful numbers.) The ideal counselor should have a degree in counseling or a related field, plus a board certificate or a state license. Briefly interview several pros by telephone to assure they are qualified to offer the specific services you're searching for—be it therapy, career development counseling, or testing. And, above all, work with someone with whom you feel comfortable.

Another alternative to consider—and one that is growing in popularity nationwide—is to hire a career coach. Virtually nonexistent as recently as 1990, an estimated eighteen hundred coaches currently advise some twenty thousand workers per year. In contrast to a career counselor, coaches are more like "job therapists," who can help you identify your best skills, define your career aspirations, devise strategies to help you earn more money, and make you more valuable to your current or next boss. Much like their counterparts in athletics, coaches also inspire you to set and achieve specific goals that will not only improve your career, but also, by extension, your life.

Come up with alternatives to switching careers if yours isn't a good fit

If you can't love your work—or switching to your dream career isn't financially feasible right now, then what? Sher recommends finding a way to pursue your passion on the side, perhaps as a volunteer, by enrolling in college courses, or even by moonlighting for a short time to see if that's really what you want to do. "Meanwhile, begin thinking of your regular job—the work you do as a means to pay the bills—as a *subsidy* to your chosen work," she says. "It's much easier to put up with a less-than-thrilling job when you're pursuing a passionate interest on the side."

Marilyn Greenwell agrees. "In college, I longed to be a theater major. But my father, who was a successful accountant—and who was also footing the bill for my education—insisted that I study business. 'There's no money in theater,' he told me, and he was probably right."

Today, as a single mother of two, Greenwell is grateful for her father's direction. "Had I gone into theater, I probably wouldn't have been able to support my family after my divorce," she admits. "But, thankfully, I make a good living working in senior management for a large restaurant chain. And while the job is often routine and predictable, I have a second job that sustains me."

Indeed, most evenings and weekends, Greenwell can be found at a community theater, where, as a volunteer, she wears a number of hats: director, scenery painter, costume designer, and even supporting actress. "I can take anything from eight to five, so long as I have this creative outlet in my life," she says. And recently, I've gotten my kids involved as well, so it's become a family affair."

Figure in finances

Another key to happiness in both career and life, according to psychotherapist Arlene Hirsch, a Chicago career counselor and author of *Love Your Work and Success Will Follow,* is to integrate financial and personal needs. "People tend to get into that either/or thing," she says. "But it's not a question of what's first—money or creativity. It's about how you meet both needs."

In other words, your best bet is to figure out exactly how much money you and your family need to live on. Then, once you know where you stand financially, you can earmark the resources you'll need to explore a new career—whether that may involve getting more training, taking a short sabbatical from your current job, or finding a lower-paying position that lets you get a foot in the door in your chosen new field.

It's also important to sort out real financial need from the tendency to use money as a measure of self-worth and happiness.

Vicki Robin, coauthor of the best-selling *Your Money or Your Life,* adds, "You need to define money as something for which you trade your life energy. Work is not just an eight- or nine-hour a day proposition for most people. It's more like twelve hours—which often doesn't include time spent traveling, nor preparing to go on the road. And don't forget to add the extra hours you sleep or rest on the weekend because you're wiped out."

In fact, Robin recommends dividing your take-home pay by the number of *real* hours spent devoted to our careers. Then decide: is your time worth that amount per hour? "Lots of people end up wondering why they run to an office in special clothes for the privilege of spending money on a big mortgage for a house they don't have time to enjoy," she notes.

Be patient

Keep in mind that sometimes finding your niche can take a lot longer than you expected. Leslie Christian's story is a case in point.

During most of the '80s—and at the height of the bull market—Christian worked as a director at Salomon Brothers, a major New York investment firm. Earning six figures, she loved the markets and the action, but was working killer hours—and in a frat house atmosphere. "The bottom line was the only measure of success," she recalls. "I devoted myself almost exclusively to my job and had no free time to get involved in nonprofits or politics, two areas I'd been particularly interested in before moving to New York."

At Christian's firm, men had all the power, and to be successful, she had to conform. "I felt stifled and never free to express myself," she reports. "And, in time, I came to realize that as a woman, I would never be fully accepted." In early 1988, Christian decided to resign from her position. "The job that had once made me feel energized—even mesmerized—had lost its allure," she explains.

A bonus, paid out over three years, allowed Christian to take her time finding her new niche. She moved back to Seattle, where she had attended college in the late '60s, and volunteered at a shelter for battered women. "That was a real eye-opener," says Christian, who eventually accepted an $8.50-per-hour job as an administrative assistant at the shelter, and stayed on for nine months.

Later, she dabbled in fund-raising for an organization concerned with AIDS and took courses in art history on the side. Job opportunities continued to come her way, but she turned them all down. "I resisted going back to work for a big company," she says. "I was afraid I wouldn't be able to direct my life again."

In February of 1991, Christian decided to combine her strong feminist views with her love for the stock market by becoming a certified financial planner. Her specialty, she decided, would be helping women gain better control of their finances. "I had no objection to making money. I just wanted to help others, too," she says. "And I liked the idea of creating a business and making it reflect who I was and what I valued."

Although successful, Christian felt too isolated working by herself. Thus, when a job offer from a large Seattle-based consulting firm came her way, she decided to accept it. "That was a big mistake. I was right back in a dog-eat-dog corporate atmosphere, and my life, once again, became unbalanced."

Christian lasted there just over two years, then joined Progressive Investment Management, a small Portland firm that specializes in socially responsible investing. Today, she is president of that company and proclaims she has finally found her niche. "I'm back in investments, which I've always found intriguing. I'm managing people and working with clients, which I've always liked. Most important, this company's values are consistent with mine. Finally, all the pieces feel good to me."

Take time to distinguish wants from needs

"If you'd met me at a party five years ago, you'd have thought I had it all," reveals Sarah Ban Breathnach, author of the phenomenally successful *Simple Abundance: A Daybook of Comfort and Joy.* "I did have a sheen of success, but I felt like a chocolate bunny—hollow inside. I had to learn to stop looking to the world for happiness and start looking within and living accordingly."

Breathnach eventually redefined success by learning to distinguish between her wants and needs. "Much of what I thought I wanted was merely excess," she discovered. "Many women don't make this distinction—they simply don't have time to think about it. Then we wonder why we feel so empty and frustrated and exhausted."

Simplicity is key to self-exploration, Breathnach adds. "And simplicity begins with giving yourself time to excavate that self and identify what you need. Then, don't be afraid to explore your passions and to honor them. It's exciting. It can be scary. But once you allow your authentic self to emerge, you won't want to go back."

Remind yourself that it's never too late to pursue a dream

A little over a decade ago, Clara Villarosa's career was humming. Having started out as a psychiatric social worker, she'd climbed the ladder to department head and hospital administrator before venturing into corporate America. There, she was thriving as a vice president of human resources and strategy planning at a large bank in Denver, Colorado. "It was an extremely seductive atmosphere, because you had all the perks—an expense account, a health plan, and the security of the corporate structure around you," she says.

Nevertheless, at the age of fifty-three, when most women are looking ahead to retirement, Villarosa decided to toss out this security blanket by quitting her job—and the $50,000 paycheck it provided her—to pursue her lifelong dream of opening a bookstore.

Always a passionate reader, Villarosa wanted to sell a product she already knew something about and that "related in a positive way to my people—the African-American community." To establish The Hue-Man Experience Bookstore (Hue-Man means man of color), Villarosa converted two row houses in Denver to create just the ambience she had in mind.

Today, her venture is the largest African-American bookstore in the country both in terms of size and titles. The business grossed $350,000 last year, and—thanks to mail order—boasts over six thousand customers on six continents. "It took a good nine years before I could declare myself financially comfortable," says Villarosa, who's now sixty-seven. "But I've learned so much, and it's been an incredibly joyful journey."

Find ways to make work—and life—meaningful

True success requires carving out a life that is personally meaningful, believes John W. Gardner, author of *Self-Renewal: The Individual and the Innovative Society.* "And meaning is not something you stumble across, like the answer to a riddle or the prize in a treasure hunt," he writes. "Meaning is something you build into your life. You build it out of your own past, out of your affections and loyalties, out of the experience of humankind as it is passed on to you, and out of your own talent and understanding, out of the things you believe in, out of the things and people you love, and out of the values for which you are willing to sacrifice something. The ingredients are there. You are the only one who can put them together into that unique pattern that will be your life."

Life is about choices—and you are what you choose, confirms Rebecca Maddox, owner of Capital Rose, Inc., and author of *Inc. Your Dreams*. "Successful people don't just fall into being successful. They create their own successes—one choice at a time."

The good news is, each of us possesses the "right stuff" to be successful—if we decide we want to use it, Maddox believes. "But I'm convinced that we only use it when we find what it is that we love to do. *That's* when we decide to call on the right stuff within us, because there's no longer any choice in the matter."

WISHING YOU ALL THE "RIGHT STUFF"

"Some people are lucky enough to know what they love from the start," Maddox adds. "Others diligently seek it out. Still others find themselves in an unexpected situation that brings forth a sense of 'That's it!' However we find it, when we do find it, we discover that we *do* have the right stuff. In essence, loving what you do opens the door."

As you rewrite *your* own script, search deep inside yourself to find *your* own right stuff. In the end, not only will you treasure the journey, you will have developed your own personal road map for success.

CHAPTER TWELVE

A Wake-Up Call for Corporate America

It is not only a question of who is responsible for very young children. There is no longer anyone home to care for adolescents and the elderly. There is no one around to take in the car for repair or to let the plumber in. Working families are faced with daily dilemmas: Who will take care of a sick child? Who will go to the big soccer game? Who will attend the teacher conference?

—FRAN SUSSNER RODGERS

When the Women's Bureau of the U.S. Department of Labor recently surveyed a quarter of a million women regarding their job-related concerns, respondents' number-one complaint was the difficulty of balancing work and family. These results are hardly surprising, considering that the number of women with children ages eighteen and under in today's workforce exceeds twenty-three million.

Granted, a majority of women—70 percent, according

to a 1997 study conducted by *Ladies' Home Journal,* in partnership with the renowned social-science research firm DYG, Inc.—say that women are better off today than they were in the past. But progress has its price. Eighty percent also believe that stress levels among women are at an all-time high, and that a major culprit is having to balance multiple roles.

TOWARD A MORE FAMILY-FRIENDLY WORKPLACE

On the plus side, burgeoning numbers of companies nationwide have begun initiating a variety of policies and programs designed to make juggling the demands of work and family easier.

Indeed, "family-friendly" appears to be among the leading buzzwords of the '90s. In 1986, when *Working Mother* magazine set out to find family-friendly companies, they struggled to compile a list of thirty firms believed to be worthy of recognition. Today, hundreds of employers actively campaign for a coveted spot on the magazine's annual roster of the "100 Best Companies for Working Mothers."

Work-family issues have managed to make their way into the political arena as well. In 1996, the White House sponsored a conference on corporate citizenship—a political first. One goal of the conference was to spotlight companies that, as President Clinton put it, "do the right thing," by offering their employees such benefits as on-site child care, flexible working hours, and paid maternity and paternity leaves. A month later, a second conference—led by Vice President Al Gore—was convened to look at how work affects families and vice versa.

WHO'S MINDING THE KIDS?

Naturally, finding quality but affordable child care is a major issue for working moms, and there's good news here as well. Companies offering assistance in this area have grown tenfold over the past decade.

For starters, postpartum blues for working mothers seems to be easing. At growing numbers of companies, new moms have generous new choices for returning more gradually to work after giving birth. In addition to job sharing, flextime, and part-time options, many women are no longer forced to rely on accrued sick and vacation days to bond with their newborns. Indeed, longer than ever—and fully paid—maternity leaves are available at such companies as J. P. Morgan (fourteen weeks), Merrill Lynch (thirteen weeks), and Salomon Brothers (twelve weeks).

Twenty-seven companies on *Working Mother*'s most recent top one hundred list provide paid leaves to new dads as well. Seventy percent offer financial aid for adoptions, and over thirty percent boast paid adoption leaves lasting up to twelve weeks.

Studies have shown that once new moms return to work, child-care worries can have adverse effects on job performance—making it difficult for them to concentrate, forcing many to take excessive time off, and leaving some no choice but to switch jobs or quit altogether.

Savvy companies recognize this and are making heroic efforts to assure parents' peace of mind while on the job. Some, for example, have set up dependent-care funds to help offset the costs of hiring top-notch care givers. Others have helped by subsidizing community child-care programs and providing reimbursement of child-care costs for business travel and overtime, as well as sick-child days as needed.

Seventy-nine of *Working Mother*'s top one hundred companies have invested big bucks to build on-site or near-site day-care centers for their employees' youngsters. Allstate Insurance Company, for example, recently spent $3 million to construct an on-site center at its headquarters in Northbrook, Illinois. Three additional near-site centers serve workers in Dallas, Charlotte, and Huntington, New York.

Some five hundred youngsters are enrolled in four child-care centers owned and operated by Florida's Barnett Banks, Inc. And with long waiting lists to take advantage of this popular benefit, the company recently allocated $4 million for the construction of a fifth center in Jacksonville.

At many firms, caring for and educating children doesn't end after the day-care years. Most companies boasting on- or near-site centers also offer afterschool, holiday, and summer programs for kids, as well as emergency backup care when parents' regular arrangements fall through.

A smattering of companies—Hewlett-Packard, Dayton Hudson, Bayfront Medical Center, American Bankers Insurance Group, and Sequent Computer Systems—even subsidize or have built on- or near-site accredited elementary schools.

HAPPINESS IS . . .

A majority of the more than twenty-three million mothers in today's workforce are there by choice. In fact, according to a recent *Working Mother* survey, when asked if they could have one wish, only 10 percent chose "being able to stay at home." Work, they say, enhances their sense of well-being, and this was true for both married and divorced moms.

But the one aspect of work that affected women's happiness the most was flexibility. Seventy percent of the happiest women surveyed said they could take time off work when they needed to, and over half said they had some choice about when they arrived and left work each day.

In contrast, unhappy respondents were almost twice as likely to say they had little or no flexibility at their jobs. In fact, flexibility was ranked so important that some women who answered the survey were willing to give up other rewards—like higher pay and bonuses—to have it.

FLEXIBILITY: THE MOST WANTED BENEFIT

The fact is, working mothers aren't the only ones longing for flexibility. According to a new study of dual career couples by Catalyst, a New York City–based research organization, both men and women—with *and* without children—said that tops on their wish lists was more control over their time.

"People aren't looking for elaborate programs. They just want more flexibility over how they work," reports Tara Levine, Catalyst's director of research and advisory services. "These couples would simply like to be able to work from home when the need arises, as well as leave work early or arrive later when necessary."

Fortunately, companies offering alternative work schedules are on the upswing nationwide. And no wonder! A recent 614-employer survey by Watson Wyatt Worldwide ranked flexible schedules as the most effective retention tool—better than training, above-market pay, and stock options. Perhaps that's why a whopping twenty-five thousand IBM employees now work from home, and at AT&T, some sixteen thousand workers telecommute.

In numerous companies, working part-time is no longer considered a career-killer, as even partners at such blue-chip firms as Price Waterhouse are now allowed to do so—and without giving up benefits. Job sharing is also encouraged by many firms. In fact, DuPont has set up a program called FlexMatch that helps staffers find job sharing opportunities.

Compressed work schedules are growing in popularity as well. Prior to 1995, a mere handful of Amoco Corporation employees worked alternative schedules, even though company guidelines offered these options. In 1996, following a successful pilot program, however, Amoco decided to allow entire business units—not just individual employees—to move to what they call 9/80 compressed schedules (eighty hours over nine days). Initially, fifty-five hundred employees switched to the new schedule; today ten thousand—or one-third of the company's workforce—enjoy this benefit. "Having an extra day to myself every other week has really helped me to restore balance in my life," says one forty-two-year-old mother of four who has worked for Amoco for nearly a decade.

ADDRESSING OTHER WORK-LIFE CONFLICTS

According to one of the most extensive studies to date on the subject, work-life conflicts reach far beyond who's minding the kids and affect virtually *all* employees, not just working moms. The joint study, conducted over eighteen months by Baxter Healthcare (which has since changed its name to Allegiance Healthcare) in Deerfield, Illinois, and MK Consultants in Evanston, Illinois, concluded that "work-life conflict is afflicting men and women, single and married people, low-income and high-income workers alike.

"Contrary to the common belief that working women with families are most pressed by demands from home, in reality, men, singles, and dual earners *without children* were among the groups most likely to have considered changing jobs because of work-life conflict," reports Alice Campbell, director of Work & Life at Allegiance and coauthor of the study.

Specifically, the study revealed that hourly workers' biggest complaint was that they got no respect. Many also resented being ordered to work overtime on short notice or to change schedules abruptly. Yet another complaint was being denied time off for arbitrary reasons.

Salaried staff, on the other hand, said they were most frustrated by not being able to find balance in their lives due to expectations for frequent evening and weekend work, plus nonstop voice-mail availability.

"These conflicts clearly affected on-the-job performance," says Campbell. "Most workers were unwilling to put in extra effort, volunteer to work overtime, or even speak positively to customers. Their reasoning: 'Why

166

should *we* bend over backward if they're not committed to us?'"

PERKS WITH BIG PAYOFFS

Recent and rampant restructuring, downsizing, and megamergers have left many of today's already frazzled employees feeling more pressured at the workplace than ever before. Greater responsibilities and opportunities to work extra hours are the last thing these burned-out survivors need. For many, even pay raises won't cut it anymore.

Fortunately, companies that realize this are beginning to offer nonmonetary perks to make work more enjoyable. At Autodesk, a San Rafael, California–based software developer, for example, employees are allowed to bring their dogs to work. Andersen Management Consulting in Chicago offers a concierge service that can be at a worker's house when the cable company comes, or can pick up an employee's car from the repair shop.

At Morningstar, a Chicago financial publishing company, employees are offered a six-week paid sabbatical every four years in addition to their annual paid vacation. "With two weeks of vacation, you're like a hamster on a wheel," believes company chairman Joe Mansueto. "A sabbatical gives you a chance to develop new skills and break out of the rut."

Xerox also boasts a sabbatical program that allows several employees every year to take paid leaves of absence—from one month to one year—and work for charitable organizations. "People often come back with skills they didn't know they had," says Joseph M. Cahalan, head of the Stamford-based Xerox Foundation, which oversees the sabbatical program.

Motorola offers a benefits package that includes a cash payment of up to $5,000 for employees who have been with the company for ten years. That money can then be spent on a shopping list of benefits ranging from gym memberships and educational opportunities, to baby-sitting or elder-care costs, and even a down payment on a new house.

At Wilson Connor Packaging, Inc., in Charlotte, North Carolina, employees can take their laundry to work—and for the cost of the soap, have it washed, dried, and folded. The company also boasts a handyman on staff who does free minor household repairs for employees while they're at work.

Finally, stressed-out employees at Quad/Graphics, a $500 million company based in Pewaukee, Wisconsin, that prints more than four hundred publications, including *Time, Newsweek,* and *Architectural Digest,* have access to a company fitness center. Massages are also available for a nominal fee.

Of course, there's a good reason behind this wave of altruism. Competition to attract—and keep—the best and brightest workers has never been keener, and companies have little choice but to go out on a limb.

After all, recent studies reveal that turnover rates have risen to their highest levels in nearly a decade. And replacing an employee costs one to one and a half times the departed worker's annual salary, according to Hewitt Associates, a Lincolnshire, Illinois, management-consulting firm. So, for this reason alone, corporations have a powerful incentive to hang on to their staff.

BATTLING IT OUT TO BE THE BEST

Indeed, raging turnover (particularly among women) and a shortage of experienced talent among the nation's largest accounting firms has recently created what the *Wall Street Journal* calls "The Battle of the Big Six." The corporate giants—Price Waterhouse, Deloitte & Touche, Arthur Andersen, Ernst & Young, Coopers & Lybrand, and KPMG—are vying to keep workers happy, reports *Journal* columnist Sue Shellenbarger. "They are competing to get on best-employer lists and are promoting a blizzard of new initiatives, from flexible schedules to novel career tracks."

Some examples: Ernst & Young has set up an innovative database on its various flexible work arrangements with 450 user profiles. Under this plan, individual employees can take a self-assessment quiz to help them determine which (if any) flexible schedule is right for them. The firm reports that the database drew seven thousand hits in its first month and has since given Ernst & Young bragging rights to having the highest percentage of flexible workers (6 percent) among the Big Six.

Ernst & Young is also piloting a plan to eliminate pointless overwork. "We're exploring ways to help our employees regain balance—by improving communication about work priorities with both partners and clients, by eliminating unnecessary pressure, and by helping people break from voice mail and e-mail during vacations," says Deborah Holmes, head of Ernst & Young's new Office of Retention.

Other firms are replacing overtime pay with salaries that match compensation to performance in meeting individual or group targets. "We've removed the idea that you have to work a lot to be successful," says Danny

Reigle, managing director of human resources and recruiting at Arthur Andersen.

PROOF IS IN THE PROFITS

The good news is, when companies make the effort to treat employees as their most valuable resource and initiate programs to help staffers lead more balanced lives, the results can be magical. Morale improves, loyalty skyrockets, and employee turnover plummets. In service-related industries, even customers benefit. More often than not, profits increase as well. Following are some examples.

- In 1996, First Tennessee Bank's overall revenue growth hit 11 percent. To put that figure in perspective, the average for the banking industry hovers between 6 and 7 percent.

  Their secret? In branches where employees' work-life needs were being met, staffers had better attitudes, which led to happier customers and higher profits. Specifically, workers were granted greater control over how they got their work done, and bank managers were encouraged to focus on an employee's performance results rather than the number of hours spent on the premises.

  In the accounting-processing department of one branch, for example, employees came up with the idea to work longer shifts at the beginning of each month—since this was their "crunch" period—in exchange for a day off during a slower period later in the month. The results? Within six months, workers had cut the number of days it took to reconcile accounts from ten days to four, thereby increasing customer satisfaction without increasing salary costs.

Studies also revealed that employees with more supportive bosses stayed with the bank 50 percent longer than other employees, saving the bank more than $1 million in turnover costs over a three-year period.

- Since Neville Industries, a 575-employee sock manufacturer in Hildebran, North Carolina, began offering a menu of work-family programs (including on-site day care, flextime, and emergency backup child care), turnover at the plant has dropped to an average of 45 percent a year—compared to an industry average ranging between 80 and 100 percent.

- In the late '80s, Aetna, Inc., was experiencing a 25 percent turnover rate among high-potential, professional women who took maternity leave and then decided not to return to their jobs. "By modifying our policies and allowing employees to return to work part-time after leave, attrition was cut by more than 50 percent," reports Michelle Carpenter, Aetna's director of Work/Life Strategies. "And within five years of instituting this new program, we saw an 88 to 90 percent retention rate of those taking leave—which translated into an annual savings for the company of over $1 million."

When Aetna Health Plans in Richmond, Virginia, decided to try out the idea of letting some employees work from home, one woman who processes medical claims increased her productivity by 24 percent in four months. "The more flexible the workplace is, the more people are going to

171

do for you," believes service center manager Bill Sanford.

- In 1995, a group of employees at Hewlett-Packard's Financial Services Center in Colorado Springs pitched the idea to management of working four ten-hour days instead of five eight-hour days. They argued that an extra day off would relieve stress and boost morale. Customer service would also improve, they insisted, since center staffers—who are responsible for processing financial transactions for the company's sixty thousand employees based all over the United States—working longer shifts would be better able to field calls from all the geographical time zones. Management agreed to test the idea, and almost immediately, productivity nearly doubled.

    This change in work schedules reaped other benefits as well. "Overtime hours were cut in half, which resulted in a 10 percent cost savings to the salary budget," reports Jerry Cashman, Hewlett-Packard's Work Options program manager. "The schedule has also helped in attracting and hiring new employees."

- A random sample of IBM employees found that work-family programs ranked twelfth out of sixteen factors in their decision to sign on with Big Blue, and sixth in their decision to stay with the company. Among top performers at the firm, however, these benefits were named the second most important reason for staying with the company.

- In addition to building an employee wellness and fitness center, American Bankers Insurance Group in Miami, Florida, has invested $1.4 million to build a satellite public school on its eighty-four-acre corporate campus. Currently 225 children of American Bankers employees are enrolled, and parents are encouraged to visit their kids at lunchtime and after school. "It helps recruit and retain good employees," says Philip Sharkey, head of the company's Human Resources department. "In fact, the company has reduced its turnover rate from 13 percent to an average of 5 percent for employees with children in the school, which—considering the costs associated with recruiting, hiring, and training new employees—should enable the company to recoup its investment in just over ten years."

- A recent study of eighteen thousand employees at Wilmington, Delaware–based DuPont confirmed a definite correlation between companies' efforts to support employees in balancing work and family responsibilities and employees' commitment to business. Specifically, in this study, employees who used DuPont's work-life programs were 45 percent more likely to "strongly agree" that they would "go the extra mile" to ensure DuPont's success.

EVERY EFFORT COUNTS

Granted, some companies don't have the resources, structure, or capability to offer a slew of benefits like massive flextime, job sharing, and on-site child-care centers. But new research by the Economic Policy Institute (EPI) reveals that companies who offer family-friendly environments—even without set policies in place—can boost worker morale and productivity.

EPI researchers Eileen Applebaum and Peter Berg recently surveyed about fifteen hundred workers at nineteen plants in the steel, apparel, and medical electronics industries. They found that informal work-family benefits, such as a supervisor being understanding about an employee leaving early to pick up a youngster from child care, also have a definite trickle-down effect. In essence, workers who believed their employer supported their need to balance work and family had a stronger commitment to the company's goals and reported less stress on the home front.

MORE AND MORE COMPANIES TAKE THE HOLISTIC APPROACH

For many workers, the boundaries between home and work life are often blurred, but studies show that when employees have support and resources on the job to help them handle personal problems, they are better able to focus on work. Perhaps that's why growing numbers of companies are enlisting the help of consultation and referral (C&R) services.

In the '80s, companies contracted with C&Rs primarily to provide resources for their workers in the areas of child care, elder care, and adoption. But today, C&Rs have broadened their scope to meet a wider array of employee needs—and as their services have expanded, so has their popularity.

LifeWorks, for example, is a C&R service run by the Boston-based consulting firm WFD. Its staff comprises 130 counselors who field some fifteen hundred calls a day (from eight offices, including one in Canada and one in the United Kingdom) from employees at companies as diverse as The Gap, Texas Instruments, and Baxter Health Care. The service features a toll-free, twenty-four-hour-a-day, seven-day-a-week telephone helpline that offers access to information on everything from legal and financial assistance to pet care, child care, marital issues, and choosing the best preschool or college. "It's not just the referrals we provide, it's the guidance and support through the whole process that makes us so popular among employees," says Karen Fischer, a LifeWorks counselor. "Once we help our clients come up with a plan that helps them feel more in control of a situation, they can concentrate on their jobs."

Companies now have access to a slew of national C&Rs that offer similar services—including WFD, Ceridian Performance Partners, Working Solutions, and DDC/The Dependent Care Connection. Collectively, these national vendors cover over twelve million workers.

Not surprisingly, employees say these services reduce stress and prevent burnout. Companies agree that they are useful, especially at impacting the bottom line. "LifeWorks saves us between fourteen and eighteen hours per employee use," estimates Nancy Poe, vice president for Work and Family at NationsBank. "We know that a portion of those hours would have been the bank's hours."

RAISING SPIRITS AT WORK

Another growing trend at American workplaces is the addition of chaplains to company payrolls. According to the National Institute of Business and Industrial Chaplains in Houston, Texas, some four thousand chaplains have recently been employed in businesses and industries nationwide.

"Business is booming," confirms Art Stricklin, director of administrative relations for Marketplace Ministries, Inc., in Dallas, whose company now has 148 business clients in thirty-four states and is adding a new one about every ten days.

But these chaplains are not being recruited to preach religion. Rather, their role is to reduce anxiety among overstressed and frustrated workers, to improve communications between employers and management, and to help disillusioned workers feel better about themselves and their jobs. "Spirituality in the workplace shows a compassionate concern and caring for employees," believes Laurie Beth Jones, author of *Jesus, CEO.* "Businesses have a tremendous capacity to help people who are suffering."

John Thomas, manager of employee services at Herr Foods, Inc., in Nottingham, Pennsylvania, agrees. His company has made chaplains available not only to the twelve hundred employees at its corporate site, but to those working at twenty-two branches spread across nine states. "What's driving our whole program is wanting employees happy and well-adjusted," Thomas says.

Chaplains in the workplace bring a sense of compassion and a personal touch to a corporate community as well. Until recently, Reverend Herb Bates was employed as one of several part-time chaplains at Hudson Specialty Foods, an 820-employee meat and poultry plant located just outside Cincinnati, Ohio. "I saw my role as providing a spiritual presence, helping to relieve stress, being a friend in the workplace, and making myself available when problems or crises came up," says the Louisville, Kentucky, native.

In his three years at Hudson, Bates has visited with ill employees in the hospital, checked in on workers or their spouses when a child was born, counseled staffers on everything from divorce to a family member's drug problem, and even performed marriage ceremonies for employees. "The better we can help people deal with their stresses and not carry them around with them, the better it is for them, and the better it is for everyone," Bates says.

Chaplains are also helping workers to find the balance so many desperately seek. At Pilgrim's Pride, a chicken processing company headquartered in Pittsburg, Texas, for example, forty chaplains serve eighty-six hundred employees at fourteen locations. "About three times each year, the chaplains give upper management a report outlining the services they have provided," says Ray Gameson, senior vice president of human resources. With their finger on the pulse of what and how workers are feeling, chaplains also provide the company with valuable insight into employees' concerns.

"Recently, the chaplains let us know that shift work was causing a lot of problems for those with small children," Gameson says. "So we got the message that we needed to look at transferring some of those people to days. The chaplains have been very good about communicating concerns with us."

If this trend continues, perhaps chaplains can provide the impetus that ultimately persuades corporations to become more conscientious in the ways they run their operations and treat their employees. After all, as Allen Cox points out in his book *Redefining Corporate Soul: Linking Purpose and People,* "For more and more people, the office has taken the place of the town meeting and the church ice cream social, becoming the place to find friends, meet mates, and initiate networks. It's where our young people learn about values and ethics and how to deal with other adults."

The bottom line, Cox concludes, is that "a company that lives its values, knows its purpose, and follows a mission can become an incubator for a caring, ethical future generation of business people and citizens."

CHAPTER THIRTEEN

Looking Ahead to the New Millennium

I took a deep breath and listened to the old brag of my heart. I am, I am, I am.

—Sylvia Plath

As we head into the twenty-first century, clearly one of the greatest challenges women face is to find ways to excel at work yet still enjoy a fulfilling personal and family life. The women's stories we've shared with you in this book prove, beyond a doubt, that this goal can be achieved. Their numbers may not be staggering for now, but we predict that as we march into the next millennium, hundreds of thousands more will join their ranks.

Indeed, a new paradigm for success is emerging, and women are at the forefront. Some are rewriting the rules altogether; others are simply realigning their priorities. Either way, slowly but surely, superwoman is dying a slow death, and in her place we find a new icon committed to reaping rich rewards beyond the bottom line.

Leading the way, of course, are the baby boomer trail-blazers—once grateful for the opportunity to get ahead, but who have burned out and become fed up with careers that have veered out of control. Fresh on their heels are throngs of Generation Xers determined to actively and intelligently create the work, workplaces, families, and lifestyles they want. As Lynn Bignell, executive recruiter of Gilbert Tweed and Associates in New York City, notes, "Gratitude has given way to a sense of entitlement."

THE CORPORATE CONNECTION

Juggling work and family isn't just a women's issue. It's become a corporate one as well, and little by little, businesses are changing their ways, too. Savvy ones are recognizing that only by valuing women and attempting to meet their changing needs will they be success stories in the next century. As management guru Tom Peters points out, "To continue to lose talented women hurts an organization severely . . . for a company without a diverse workforce is at a crippling disadvantage in today's world."

Moreover, as corporations begin to look beyond the bottom line, ultimately they discover that creating policies and programs that respond to women's needs isn't just a nice thing to do, it also enables them to thrive. And, in time, this realization will lead other companies to jump on the bandwagon as well.

AS YOU EMBARK ON YOUR JOURNEY TO SUCCESS

This book is filled with different scenarios for success, and yours will be different still. In fact, as you create your own new game plan, one of the most important messages we hope to leave you with is that success is no longer one-size-fits-all. Rather, redefining success for the twenty-first century is all about having the freedom— and luxury—to decide what success means to you.

As you figure out which elements make up your own formula, tap into the resources we've included at the end of this book for inspiration and guidance. Also, keep in mind that sometimes it takes several tries before you can find the right answer, and along the way, you will likely learn a lot by trial and error.

Remember, too, that redefining success is not necessarily about abandoning goals. Rather, it's about asking yourself tough questions like "What's my legacy?" and doing all you can to create a more balanced and joyful life. Nor is redefining success about giving up (or even reducing your level of) compensation. Rather, it's about doing what you love and feel most passionate about. In fact, interestingly enough, to write *Getting Rich Your Own Way*, researcher Srully Blotnick conducted an intriguing study. He divided fifteen hundred people into two groups and followed them for twenty years. Group A comprised 1,245 individuals (or 83 percent of the sample), all of whom were embarking on a career they had chosen primarily to make as much money as possible— and as quickly as possible. Group B, on the other hand, was made up of 255 individuals for whom money wasn't a top priority. Instead, they chose their career paths based on what they truly wanted to do.

This study's resulting data may surprise you. After twenty years, 101 of the fifteen hundred subjects had become millionaires, and all but one—or 100 out of 101—were from Group B! It just goes to show that while money may not be enough—especially if it means sacrificing a sense of balance and joy in life—if you can find a way to redefine success by doing what you love, the money may follow anyway.

Enjoy the journey!

References

SECTION ONE
Looking for Success in All the Wrong Places

CHAPTER ONE
A Time of Reckoning

Joyner, T., and M. Geewax. "Women at work." *Atlanta Journal-Constitution,* July 28, 1996, D1.

MacFarquhor, E. "Changing times." *U.S. News & World Report,* June 6, 1994, 75(2).

CHAPTER TWO
The Evolution of Superwoman

Brownlee, S. "The importance of being first." *Working Woman,* November–December 1996, 22(3).

Harte, S. "Equality a long row to hoe." *Atlanta Journal-Constitution,* July 28, 1996, D4.

————. "Women who work it out." *Atlanta Journal-Constitution,* July 29, 1996, C1.

Hubbard, K. "Her own true thing: Star columnist with a dazzling future, Anna Quindlen, chucks it all to write fiction." *People Weekly,* October 17, 1994, 104(4).

Joyner, T., and M. Geewax. "Women at work." *Atlanta Journal-Constitution,* July 28, 1996, D1.

Labrich, K., and S. E. William. "Breaking away to go on your own." *Fortune,* December 17, 1990, 40(7).

MacFarquhor, E. "Changing times." *U.S. News & World Report,* June 6, 1994, 75(2).

Morris, B. "Executive women confront midlife crisis." *Fortune,* September 18, 1995, 60(8).

Morris, M. "Reinventing your life." *Executive Female,* September–October 1992, 64(6).

"Ms. Magazine celebrates 25 years." *Athens Banner-Herald,* September 17, 1997, 9A.

Peters, D. J. "Women executives gain ground, but pay lags." *New York Daily News,* June 30, 1993, B1.

Quindlen, A. "Why I quit." *Working Woman,* December 1995, 30(3).

Shellenbarger, S. "Executive women make major gains in pay and status." *Wall Street Journal,* June 30, 1993, A3.

"Then and now: How are we doing?" *Ms.,* September–October 1997, 22(6).

Vennochi, J. "Negotiating for the life you want." *Working Woman,* May 1994, 56(6).

"A woman for the times." *Psychology Today,* September–October 1994, 26(4).

Wylie, J. *Chances and Choices: How Women Can Succeed in Today's Knowledge-Based Businesses.* Vienna, Virginia: EBW Press, 1996.

CHAPTER THREE

When Having It All Isn't Enough

Condor, B. "Never done: Women who can't draw the line end up drawn and lined." *Chicago Tribune,* December 15, 1996, C3.

Ehrenreich, B. "In search of a simpler life." *Working Woman,* December 1995, 27(4).

Kagan, J. "Success: Not what it used to be." *Working Woman,* November 1992, 54(3).

Kleiman, C. "Executives seek more family time." *Atlanta Journal-Constitution,* September 8, 1996, R3.

Kruger, P. "Superwoman's daughters." *Working Woman,* May 1994, 60(7).

Kushner, H. *When All You've Ever Wanted Isn't Enough.* New York: Pocket Books, 1987.

Marks, J. "Time out." *U.S. News & World Report,* December 11, 1995, 84(4).

Morris, B. "Executive women confront midlife crisis." *Fortune,* September 18, 1995, 60(8).

"The new status symbols." *New Woman,* April 1997, 49(1).

O'Toole, P. "Reaching for more: How people are taking the best parts of their lives to make a better whole." *Working Woman,* November 1993, 50(6).

Povich, L. "Measures of success." *Working Woman,* November 1993 6(1).

Schor, J. B. *The Overworked American: The Unexpected Decline of Leisure.* New York: Basic Books, 1993.

Shellenbarger, S. "Work & Family: New job hunters ask recruiters, 'Is there life after work?'" *Wall Street Journal,* January 29, 1997, B1.

SECTION TWO
Rewards Beyond the Bottom Line: Tales of Women Who Are Redefining Success on Their Own Terms

CHAPTER FOUR
All Work and No Play: Exiting the Rat Race

"Are you working too hard?" *Glamour,* October 1997, 248(1).

Deogun, N. "Top Pepsico executive picks family over job." *Wall Street Journal,* September 24, 1997, B1.

Eaton, L. "Is there life after Wall Street? Tales of the players who quit the game." *New York Times,* January 29, 1998, D1.

"FDIC chief resigning to be with family." *Atlanta Journal-Constitution,* March 15, 1997, E3.

Grant, P. "Chucking it all." *New Woman,* October 1996, 138(3).

Hubbard, K. "Her own true thing: Star columnist with a dazzling future, Anna Quindlen, chucks it all to write fiction." *People Weekly,* October 17, 1994, 107(4).

Joyner, T., and M. Geewax. "Women at work." *Atlanta Journal-Constitution,* July 28, 1996, D1.

Kempner, M. "Cooking up a new career." *Atlanta Journal-Constitution,* July 27, 1997, E1.

Kim, J., and C. Diaz. "Charitable gifts on the rise." *USA Today,* June 25, 1997, 2B.

Kretchmar, L. "Microsoft's secret weapon." *Working Woman,* July 1995, 52(4).

Maney, K. "Stonesifer finally finds exit at Microsoft." *USA Today,* October 30, 1996, 2B.

McKenna, E. P. *When Work Doesn't Work Anymore.* New York: Delacorte Press, 1997.

"Microsoft's interactive media chief quitting." *Atlanta Journal-Constitution,* October 30, 1996, D2.

Morris, M. "Reinventing your life." *Executive Female,* September 1992, 64(6).

Niswander, R. "I escaped the rat race." *McCall's,* June 1997, 61(1).

Quindlen, A. "Why I quit." *Working Woman,* December 1995, 30(3).

Schor, J. B. *The Overworked American: The Unexpected Decline of Leisure.* New York: Basic Books, 1997.

Shellenbarger, S. "Work & Family: Woman's resignation from top Pepsi post rekindles debates." *Wall Street Journal,* October 8, 1997, B1.

Singletary, M. "FDIC chairwoman to resign in June." *Washington Post,* March 15, 1997, C1.

"A woman for the times." *Psychology Today,* September–October 1994, 26(4).

CHAPTER FIVE

Plateauing on Purpose

"Black women firsts: Hidden gems of black history." *Ebony,* April 1997, 79(3).

References

"Dr. Ruth Simmons named ninth president of prestigious Smith College." *Jet,* January 9, 1995, 25(1).

Edwards, A. "Ruth Simmons: College president." *Essence,* August 1996, 40(1).

Joyner, T. "Keeping the corps: As turnover rises, companies are using innovative techniques to retain workers." *Atlanta Journal-Constitution,* November 9, 1997, P1.

Martinez, M. N. "The proof is in the profits." *Working Mother,* May 1997, 27(4).

Morris, B. "Executive women confront midlife crisis." *Fortune,* September 18, 1995, 60(8).

Picker, L. "The key to my success." *Parade Magazine,* April 21, 1996, 4(2).

Shellenbarger, S. "Work and Family: One entrepreneur who shapes success to fit family needs." *Wall Street Journal,* September 18, 1996, B1.

Swiss, D. J., and J. P. Walker. "Fast track moms." *Executive Female,* November–December 1993, 44(5).

Townsel, L. J. "Dr. Ruth J. Simmons: First sister to head a Seven-Sister school." *Ebony,* June 1996, 94(3).

Vennochi, J. "Negotiating for the life you want." *Working Woman,* May 1994, 56(6).

CHAPTER SIX

Backtracking: You Can Go Home Again

Brogden, L. "The no that saved my soul." *MomsOnline.* Internet article.

Conlin, J. "Sailing in and out of a career." *Working Woman,* December 1995, 46(4).

Deutschman, A. "Pioneers of the new balance: More managers are striking deals for flexible work schedules. They have more time for their kids and—surprise—their careers are prospering." *Fortune,* May 20, 1991, 60(5).

Dolan, K. "Fairfield bound? Deborah Coleman is Merix Corporation's CEO." *Forbes,* February 27, 1995, 142(1).

Hemley, F. M. "Good, better, best." *Working Woman,* December 1987, 86(4).

Hyatt, J. "The zero-defect CEO." *Inc.,* June 1997, 46(8).

REFERENCES

CHAPTER SEVEN
The Joy Crisis: Caring for Our Souls

Bamford, J. "America's top 50 women business owners." *Working Woman,* May 1994, 39(13).

Bassett, L. *From Panic to Power: Proven Techniques to Calm Your Anxieties, Conquer Your Fears, and Put You in Control of Your Life.* New York: HarperCollins, 1997.

Bond, P. "A new course in back to school." *Atlanta Journal-Constitution,* July 29, 1996, C5.

Canfield, J., and J. Miller. *Heart at Work: Stories and Strategies for Building Self-Esteem and Reawakening the Soul at Work.* New York: McGraw-Hill, 1996.

Capen, R., Jr., *Finish Strong.* New York: HarperCollins/Zondervan Publishers, 1996.

De Angelis, B., Ph.D. *Real Moments.* New York: Dell, 1994.

Edwards, A. "Leaving the corporate nest." *Executive Female,* July–August 1992, 32(6).

"Emptiness lies at the heart of some successful women." *Atlanta Journal-Constitution,* June 12, 1996, D12.

Kushner, H. *When All You Ever Wanted Isn't Enough.* New York: Pocket Books, 1987.

Nelson, A. J., N. Stesin, L. Harris, and B. B. Burgower. "Get a life: How five women made major changes—and succeeded." *Working Woman,* November 1993, 56(6).

Schindehette, S., and U. Wihlborg. "Reel to real." *People Weekly,* January 26, 1998, 71(2).

Sipp, C. "Trading trappings for ties that bind." *Atlanta Journal-Constitution,* July 29, 1996, C5.

CHAPTER EIGHT
Boredom Not Burnout: When the Thrill Is Gone

Csikszentmihalyi, M. *Finding Flow: The Psychology of Engagement with Everyday Life.* New York: Basic Books, 1997.

Friedman, L. "Sick of your job?" *New Woman,* October 1996, 170(4).

Griffin, K. "What I did for love." *Working Woman,* December 1995, 38(6).

188

References

Morris, M. "Reinventing your life." *Executive Female,* September–October 1992, 64(6).

Moses, N. "Manager's Journal: The nonprofit motive." *Wall Street Journal,* March 17, 1997, A18.

CHAPTER NINE

Postpartum Blues: Putting an End to the Tug-of-War

Alexander, J. "Getting your job done from home: Telecommuting lets you keep your benefit and your paycheck." *Money,* March 1996, 80(1).

Bamford, J. "How women meet the challenge of managing divided lives for multiplied blessing." *Bloomberg Personal Archives,* November 1995. Internet article.

Blakely, S. "Women entrepreneurs." *Nation's Business,* June 1997, 74(1).

Farrell, W. "Behind the pay gap." Letter to editor. *Wall Street Journal,* September 16, 1997, A23.

Gage, A. "The ultimate job share: This couple shares a marriage, a home, a child, and an office at American Express." *The St. Paul Pioneer Press,* January 5, 1997, 6D.

"Home-based women-owned businesses number and employ millions." National Foundation for Women Business Owners. Press release. November 16, 1995.

Hugg, P. *101 Best Home-Based Businesses for Women.* Rocklin, Calif.: Prima Publications, 1995.

Joyner, T., and M. Geewax. "Women at work." *Atlanta Journal-Constitution,* July 28, 1996, D1.

"In the News: Putting family first." *First for Women,* October 10, 1997, 80(1).

Lawlor, J. "Bottom line on work-family programs." *Working Woman,* July–August 1996, 54(6).

Link Resources Corporation. *National Work-at-Home Survey,* 1996.

Matson, M. "Working mothers: These make the best of both worlds." *Good Housekeeping,* March 1989, 46(3).

Micco, L. "Employees may prefer pajamas in new workplace trend." *HR News Online.* Internet article.

Molinari, S. "A mother's choice: Why I left Congress." *Family Circle,* November 16, 1997, 152(1).

Morris, Michele. "Career control: How it gets four women the work and lives they want." *Executive Female,* November–December 1991, 26(4).

Munk, N., and S. Oliver. "Women of the valley." *Forbes,* December 30, 1996, 102(6).

Nelton, S. "Capital ideas for financing." *Nation's Business,* September 1996, 18(8).

"New national survey reports sharp rise in telecommuting." Press release, Telecommute America, July 2, 1997.

Olsen, H. "Getting a handle on flextime." *Working Woman,* February 1996, 55(3).

Robaton, A. "Banking on women." *Working Woman,* November 1997, 66(3).

Schlesinger, G. B. "In a hurry." In J. Canfield, M. V. Hansen, J. R. Hawthorne, and M. Shimoff, *Chicken Soup for the Woman's Soul: 101 Stories to Open the Hearts and Rekindle the Spirits of Women.* Deerfield Beach, Fla.: Hearth Communications, 1996.

Shapiro, L. "The myth of quality time." *Newsweek,* May 12, 1997, 62(8).

Smalley, B. S. "Earn $35,000, $50,000, $100,000 a year working at home." *Woman's World,* September 30, 1997, 16(2).

CHAPTER TEN

Passion with a Purpose: Doing Well by Doing Good

Aburdene, P., and J. Naisbitt. *Megatrends for Women.* New York: Villard Books, 1992.

Brady, J. "In step with Oprah Winfrey." *Parade Magazine,* October 26, 1997, 12(1).

Clarke, K. "Do we have any volunteers?" *Sky,* June 1997, 121(3).

Darlin, D. "Full-court press." *Forbes,* March 24, 1997, 80(1).

Dodd, K. "Haven offers help to women, kids with AIDS." Special Supplement to the *Kansas City Business Journal,* May 30, 1997, 13(1).

Dziemianowicz, J., and Z. Kashef. "The Oprah you don't know." *McCall's,* August 1995, 72(4).

Gramig, M. H. "Executive paves the way for other women." *Atlanta Journal-Constitution,* March 2, 1997, G5.

Heller, M. "A call for help." *Lear's,* December 1993, 65(2).

Kanner, M. "Oprah at 40: What she's learned the hard way." *Ladies' Home Journal,* February 1994, 96(6).

Lyons, P. "Doing good by doing well." *Ladies' Home Journal,* September 1994, 112(4).

Maddox, R. *Inc. Your Dreams.* New York: Viking Penguin, 1996.

"Muriel Siebert: First woman of finance." Web site biography (http:www.msiebert.com/bio.htm).

Noglows, P. "Oprah: The year of living dangerously." *Working Woman,* May 1994, 52(5).

Petzinger, Jr., T. "The front lines: Nurse agency thrives by taking hard cases in the inner city." *Wall Street Journal,* September 26, 1997, B1.

Plitch, P. "Wall Street pioneer Muriel Siebert is still making a mark with new deals." *Wall Street Journal,* May 27, 1997, A13.

Smith, L. "Oprah exhales." *Good Housekeeping,* October 1998, 120(6).

SECTION THREE
Finding Solutions for Work-Life Conflicts

CHAPTER ELEVEN
To Thine Own Self Be True: Rewriting Your Own Script

Breathnach, S. B. *Simple Abundance: A Daybook of Comfort and Joy.* New York: Warner Books, 1995.

Dominguez, J., and V. Robin. *Your Money or Your Life: Transforming Your Relationship with Money and Achieving Financial Independence.* New York: Penguin Books, 1992.

Friedman, L. "Sick of your job?" *New Woman,* October 1996, 170(3).

Gardner, J. W. *Self Renewal: The Individual and the Innovative Society.* New York: W. W. Norton, 1995.

Griffin, K. "What I did for love." *Working Woman,* December 1995, 38(6).

Hirsch, A. *Love Your Work and Success Will Follow: A Practical Guide to Achieving Total Career Satisfaction.* New York: John Wiley & Sons, 1996.

Maddox, R. *Inc. Your Dreams.* New York: Viking Penguin, 1996.

Morris, B. "Executive women confront midlife crisis," *Fortune,* September 18, 1995, 60(8).

Pagano, B. L. "Baby boomers redefining success." *Atlanta Journal-Constitution,* December 12, 1993, D3.

Sher, B. *Live the Life You Love.* New York: Delacorte, 1996.

————. *I Could Do Anything If I Only Knew What It Was.* New York: Delacorte, 1995.

CHAPTER TWELVE
A Wake-Up Call for Corporate America

Brothers, P. "Chaplains take ministry to temples of industry." *Cincinnati Enquirer,* April 12, 1997, C3.

Bruzzese, A. "Divine Intervention." *Human Resource Executive,* May 20, 1997, 1(4).

Cassidy, A. "Happy: Who is happy? 1000 moms reveal their secrets for enjoying life." *Working Mother,* November 1995, 27(4).

Costello, M. "Dealing with downshifters." *Working Woman,* December 1995, 19(3).

Cox, A., with J. Liesse. *Redefining Corporate Soul: Linking Purpose and People.* Burr Ridge, Ill.: Irwin Professional Publishing, 1996.

Dolan, K. A. "When money isn't enough." *Forbes,* November 18, 1996, 164(6).

Harper, T. "An effort worth duplicating." *Sky,* April 1997, 81(4).

Harris, D. "Big business takes on child care." *Working Woman,* June 1993, 50(5).

Harte, S. "Women who work it out." *Atlanta Journal-Constitution,* July 29, 1995, C1.

Hutter, S. "The problem solvers." *Working Mother,* March 1998, 34(3).

"In the family-friendly mood." *Working Mother,* February 1998, 12(1).

Jones, L. B. *Jesus, CEO: Using Ancient Wisdom for Visionary Leadership.* New York: Hyperion, 1996.

Kleiman, C. "Executives seek more family time." *Atlanta Journal-Constitution,* September 8, 1996, R3.

Lawlor, J. "The bottom line on work-family programs." *Working Woman,* July–August 1996, 54(5).

References

Marks, J. "Time out: Plagued by stress, a growing number of people say they think time is becoming more precious than money and they're trying to slow down." *U.S. News & World Report,* December 11, 1995, 84(8).

Martinez, M. N. "The proof is in the profits." *Working Mother,* May 1997, 27(4).

Moskowitz, M. "12th Annual Survey of 100 Best Companies for Working Mothers." *Working Mother,* October 1997, 19(37).

———. "11th Annual Survey of 100 Best Companies for Working Mothers." *Working Mother,* October 1996, 10(33).

———, and C. Townsend. "Tenth anniversary: 100 Best Companies for Working Mothers." *Working Mother,* October 1995, 18(36).

"The most-wanted benefit." *Parenting,* March 1998, 69(1).

Shellenbarger, S. "Work and family: Accounting firms battle to be known as best work places." *Wall Street Journal,* January 21, 1998, B1.

———. "Work and family issues go way beyond missed ball games." *Wall Street Journal,* May 20, 1997, B1.

Willis, C. "The 10 most admired women managers in America." *Working Woman,* December 1993, 44(11).

CHAPTER THIRTEEN
Looking Ahead to the New Millennium

"Do what you love—the money will follow." In J. Canfield and J. Miller, *Heart at Work.* New York: McGraw-Hill, 1996.

Lawlor, J. "Executive exodus." *Working Woman,* November 1994, 39(4).

O'Toole, P. "Reaching for more: How people are taking the best parts of their lives to make a better whole." *Working Woman,* November 1993, 50(6).

Resources

CHAPTER SIX
Backtracking: You Can Go Home Again

The Partnership Group
Beth McCarty
211 W. Wacker, Suite 1375
Chicago, IL 60606
Phone: (312) 422-7727
Fax: (312) 422-8415

This firm works with companies nationwide to help them develop workforce effectiveness programs, including LifeBalance®, a resources and support service for employees.

CHAPTER SEVEN
The Joy Crisis: Caring for Our Souls

Shoya Zichy
Career Counselor and Consultant
New York, NY 10021
Phone: (212) 755-2849
E-mail: ShoyaN@aol.com

Zichy specializes in career and vocational testing and counseling.

Midwest Center for Stress and Anxiety, Inc.
Lucinda Bassett
Corporate Office:
106 N. Church St., Suite 200
P.O. Box 205
Oak Harbor, OH 43449
Phone: (800) 944-9428; (419) 898-4357
Fax: (419) 898-0669
Web Site: http://www.stresscenter.com

California office:
29350 W. Pacific Coast Highway, Suite 4B
Phone: (310) 589-3180
Fax: (310) 589-3183

For a free information packet, call (800) 944-9440.

The Sane Mother®
Carey Sipp
Atlanta, GA
Phone: (401) 352-9840
Fax: (404) 352-9842
E-mail: sanemother@aol.com

This company offers books, self-help tapes, and other products aimed at today's pressured moms, particularly single ones.

CHAPTER NINE
Postpartum Blues: Putting an End to the Tug-of-War

International Telework Association
204 E. Street, NE
Washington, DC 20002
Phone: (202) 547-6157
Fax: (202) 546-3289
Web site: http://www.telecommute.org/

A nonprofit organization devoted to promoting the economic, social, and environmental benefits of teleworking. Hosts conferences and publishes a quarterly newsletter.

Wells Fargo Bank Women's Lending Program

A $1 billion loan fund earmarked for women-owned businesses. Minimum loan is $5,000; maximum is $25,000. To qualify, an applicant must have good personal and business credit histories, two years of experience in her field, and an established account for her business. For more information, contact:
Wells Fargo Bank: (800) 359-3557, ext. 120
or
National Association of Women Business Owners: (301) 608-2590

Resources

Bank of America/Women Incorporated

A commitment from Bank of America to lend $10.6 billion to small businesses over three years. For more information, contact:
Women Incorporated: (800) 930-3993

Chase Manhattan Bank

Offers a toll-free lending hotline for women business owners in New York and New Jersey. Call (888) 588-2427.

Barnett Bank/National Association of Women Business Owners of Florida

Barnett Bank has pledged to lend $500 million to women-owned companies in Florida and Georgia. For more information, call (888) 629-2635.

U.S. Small Business Administration
Office of Women's Business Ownership
409 Third Street SW
Washington, DC 20416
Phone: (800) 8-ASK-SBA; (202) 205-6673
Web site: http://www.sbaonline.sba.gov/womeninbusiness

Contact the SBA for a guide to nationwide banks with the best record of serving small and women-owned businesses.

Dun & Bradstreet
Minority and Women-Owned Business Development Group
(800) 999-3867, ext. 6988

Call to add your name to this company's database of women-owned firms. D&B charges customers who buy this information, but does not charge businesses to be listed.

HR2000
David and Peggy Andrews
3006 NE Arthur St.
Minneapolis, MN 55418
Phone: (612) 788-9302
E-mail: HR2000INC@aol.com

In addition to heading up work-family seminars entitled "Creating a Life That Works for You," HR2000 specializes in leadership development consulting designed to prepare companies for the next millennium.

Other Resources for Female Entrepreneurs and Women-Owned Businesses

African-American Women Business Owners Association
3363 Alden Place, NE
Washington, DC 20019
Phone/Fax: (202) 399-3645

AAWBOA is open to any type of business. Benefits include financial support and information, emotional support, a free subscription to Black Enterprise *magazine, and networking with other businesses and possible customers/clients.*

American Women's Economic Development Corporation
(AWED)
71 Vanderbilt Ave., Room 320
New York, NY 10169
Phone: (800) 321-6962

AWED offers courses and training to entrepreneurs and can also assist in writing business proposals.

Association of Black Women Entrepreneurs
P.O. Box 3933
Silver Spring, MD 20911-3933
Phone: (301) 565-0527

A membership organization providing networking, referrals, seminars, and a newsletter.

BizWomen
560 W. 43 St., Suite 10M
New York, NY 10036
Web site: http://www.bizwomen.com/

The motto of this award-winning Web site is "bringing business women from all over the world together." Offers opportunities to communicate, network, exchange ideas, and provide support for one another via the Internet. Make your presence known by adding your on-line "business card," or include your products and services in the interactive catalog. Membership is free.

Resources

HR News Online
Society for Human Resources Management
1800 Duke St.
Alexandria, VA 22314
Phone: (703) 548-3440
Fax: (703) 548-9140
Web site: http://www.shrm.org/hrnews/articles

A rich resource of work-related articles, especially pertaining to alternative work schedules. Society provides its members with educational and informational services, hosts conferences and seminars, and sponsors government and media presentations and publications.

Idea Cafe
Web site: http://www.ideacafe.com

This is the Internet's "small business channel," providing a fun approach to serious business. A great site for networking among entrepreneurs.

IVillage.com: The Women's Network
Web site: http://www.ivillage.com (or AOL keyword: ivillage)

You can network with 600,000 other women without leaving your home or desk at this spacious Web site. Features include chat rooms, message boards, informative "how to" articles and expert commentary. Also, check out this site's popular book club, where members' recommendations comprise Top 10 lists.

Moneyhunter
Web site: http://www.moneyhunter.com

This on-line companion to MoneyHunt TV *provides fund-raising information for small business owners. Their goal is to entertain, educate, and empower entrepreneurs who seek capital to start, buy, or grow a business. Almost all services offered are free.*

National Association for Female Executives (NAFE)
135 West 50th St., 16th Floor
New York, NY 10020
Phone: (212) 445-6235.

Fax: (212) 445-6228
Web site: http://www.nafe.com

The nation's largest business women's organization provides a host of resources for the entrepreneur and small business owner. Offers cost-effective group benefits, valuable discounts, and financial planning services. Two hundred local chapters provide members with networking support and mentoring opportunities.

National Association of Women Business Owners (NAWBO)
1100 Wayne Ave., Suite 830
Silver Spring, MD 20910
Information Service Line: (800) 55-NAWBO
Phone: (301) 608-2590
Fax: (301) 608-2596
Web site: http://www.nawbo.org

A membership organization offering vast resources including networking contacts to women who have been in business one year or more.

National Foundation for Women Business Owners (NFWBO)
1100 Wayne Ave., Suite 830
Silver Spring, MD 20910-5603
Phone: (301) 495-4975
Fax: (301) 495-4979
Web site: http://www.nfwbo.org

The NFWBO is a nonprofit research and leadership development foundation affiliated with the National Association of Women Business Owners. It supports the growth of women business owners and their organizations through the gathering and sharing of knowledge. NFWBO's Web site offers a wealth of information and statistics on women business owners.

Small Business Development for Women
Sheila Robbins
4637 Park Dr., Suite 12
Carlsbad, CA 92008
Phone: (619) 434-7529
Fax: (619) 434-9316
E-mail: sheilarobb@aol.com

A training and consulting company founded by professional speaker, trainer, and small business expert Sheila Robbins, this organization offers entrepreneurs and small business owners expert, practical methods for achieving growth and profit.

Women Incorporated
2049 Century Park E., Suite 1100
Los Angeles, CA 90067
Phone: (800) 930-3993
Fax: (301) 277-1979
Web site: http://www.womeninc.com

A national, nonprofit membership organization whose primary goals are to improve access to capital for women entrepreneurs, provide a variety of services and benefits for its members, educate its constituency, and improve the business environment for women business owners and the business community at large, regardless of size.

Women's Resource Directory
P.O. Box 66796
Houston, TX 77266
Phone: (281) 242-0908
Fax: (281) 242-9578
Web site: http://www.ghgcorp.com/wordweb

A Web site that includes a classified directory of women-owned businesses as well as entrepreneurial resources for starting and growing your own business. Be sure to check out the Word Business Digest *here, an on-line monthly magazine filled with articles for and by women in the business world.*

CHAPTER TEN
Passion with a Purpose: Doing Well by Doing Good

New York Cares
116 E. 16th St., #6
New York, NY 10003-2112
Phone: (212) 228-5000
Web site: http://www.ny.cares.org

Involve your company or yourself. Every month, New York Cares creates more than 2,000 opportunities for New Yorkers to reach out a helping hand to their neighbors in need. Offers flexible hours and schedules for all volunteers.

PowerLink, Inc.
Barb Moore
305 Jefferson Dr.
Pittsburgh, PA 15228

Sets up advisory boards that work with women-owned businesses on a voluntary basis for one year.

Capital Rose, Inc.
Rebecca Maddox, President
1700 Market St.
Philadelphia, PA 19103-3984
Phone: (215) 246-2500
Fax: (215) 299-4584
Web site: http://www.capital.rose.com

This company provides female entrepreneurs with access to financing, information, and related products and also collaborates with Fortune 500 clients to capitalize on the growing opportunities in the women's market. In addition to The Capital Rose Perpetual Fund, a $40 million fund to finance women-owned businesses, the company's services include business plan reviews and consulting by a team of professionals.

Business for Social Responsibility
609 Mission St., 2nd Floor
San Francisco, CA 94105-3506
Phone: (415) 537-0888
Fax: (415) 537-0889
Web site: http://www.bsr.org/

A membership organization founded in 1992 for companies of all sizes and sectors, BSR's mission is to help its member companies achieve long-term commercial success by implementing policies and practices that honor high ethical standards and meet their responsibilities to all who are impacted by their decisions. BSR boasts over 1,200 members, including big names like Arthur Andersen & Co., AT&T, The Coca-Cola Company, DuPont, Merck, Ford Motor Company, Levi Strauss & Co., Marriott International, SC Johnson & Son, Inc., and Time Warner.

Resources

To Thine Own Self Be True: Rewriting Your Own Script

Barbara L. Pagano, Ed.S.
Speaker and Executive Development Consultant
4407 Southside Drive
Gulf Breeze, FL 32561
Phone: (888) 865-0923; (805) 916-1129
Fax: (850) 934-8387
E-mail: Bpagano@aol.com
Web site: http://www.execpath.com

Working from the Heart
Jacqueline McMakin, Career Counselor
1309 Merchant Lane
McLean, VA 22101-2413
Phone: (703) 827-2742
Fax: (703) 827-2289

McMakin specializes in helping women redefine success on their own terms.

Barbara Sher
Therapist and Career Counselor
New York, NY
Phone: (212) 222-6973
Fax: (212) 662-0452

In addition to offering therapy and counseling services, Sher heads up "Success Teams," groups of (primarily) women who meet on a regular basis to discuss and find ways to help each other's dreams come true. There is no charge to join this group.

National Board for Certified Counselors, Inc.
3 Terrace Way, Suite D
Greensboro, NC 27403-3660
Phone: (910) 547-0607
Fax: (910) 547-0017
Web site: http://www.nbcc.org

National Career Development Association
317 Kertess Avenue
Worthingon, OH 43805
Phone: (888) 326-1750

Arlene Hirsch
Career Counselor
431 S. Dearborn
Chicago, IL 60605
Phone: (312) 461-1065

Progressive Investment Management
Leslie Christian
2435 S.W. Fifth Avenue
Portland, OR 97201
Phone: (800) PROGRESS; (503) 224-7828
Fax: (503) 224-5633
or
200 First Avenue West, Suite 204
Seattle, WA 98119
Phone: (800) 366-1055; (206) 340-1055
Fax: (206) 216-0106

Progressive seeks to invest in companies that meet specific criteria for demonstrating corporate responsibility.

Career Coaching/Coaches

Acorn Business Coaching
27 Central Street
Acton, MA 01720
Phone: (508) 263-5393
Fax: (508) 263-0398

Coach University
P.O. Box 881696
Steamboat Springs, CO 80488-1595
Phone: (800) 482-6224
Fax: (800) 329-5655
Web site: http://www.coachu.com

Peer Resources Consulting Services
1052 Davie Street
Victoria, B.C., Canada V8S 4E3
Phone: (800) 567-3700 within Canada; (250) 595-3503 outside
Canada
E-mail: rcarr@islandnet.com

Resources

Success Unlimited Network
5620 Chemin De Vie, NE
Atlanta, GA 30342
Phone/Fax: (404) 851-1526
E-mail: larleen.sun@mcione.com

The Coaches Training Institute
1879 Second Street
San Rafael, CA 94901
Phone: (800) 691-6008; (415) 451-6000
Fax: (415) 460-6878
Web site: http://www.thecoaches.com

The International Coach Federation
P.O. Box 1393
Angel Fire, NM 87710
Phone: (888) 423-3131
Fax: (888) 329-2423
Web site: http://www.coachfederation.org

The Professional and Personal Coaches Association
P.O. Box 2838
San Francisco, CA 94126
Phone: (415) 522-8789
Web site: http://www.pppca.com

CHAPTER TWELVE
A Wake-Up Call for Corporate America

Results: 12th Annual Survey of Best 100 Companies for Working Mothers (For details on each company's benefits, check *Working Mother* magazine, October 1997. To order copies of back issues, call (800) 925-0788.)

Allstate Insurance
  Company*
American Management
  Systems
Amgen
Amoco Corporation
Arnold & Porter
AT&T Corp.
Avon Products, Inc.

Bankers Trust New York
  Corp.
Barnett Banks, Inc.*
Eddie Bauer, Inc.
Bayfront Medical Center,
  Inc.
Ben & Jerry's Homemade,
  Inc.
The Benjamin Group, Inc.

Beth Israel Deaconess Medical Ctr.
BP Exploration (Alaska) Inc.
The Bureau of National Affairs
Leo Burnett Company, Inc.
Calvert Group
Chase Manhattan Bank
Chrysler Corporation
Cigna Corporation
Cinergy Corp.
Citicorp/Citibank
CMP Media Inc.
Computer Associates International, Inc.
Coopers & Lybrand, LLP
Corning Incorporated
Dayton Hudson Corporation
Deloitte & Touche
DuPont Company
The DuPont Merck Pharmaceutical Co.
Eastman Kodak Company
Fel-Pro Incorporated*
First Chicago NBD Corporation
First Tennessee Bank
Ford Motor Company
The Gallup Organization
Gannett Co., Inc.
Genentech, Inc.
General Motors Corporation
Glaxo Wellcome Inc.*
Hallmark Cards, Inc.
John Hancock Mutual Life Insurance Co.
Hewlett-Packard Company

Hill, Holliday, Connors, Cosmonulos, Inc.
IBM*
Johnson & Johnson*
Johnson Wax
KPMG Peat Marwick LLP
Lancaster Laboratories
Life Technologies, Inc.
Eli Lilly and Company
Lincoln National Corporation
Lotus Development Corporation
Lucasfilm Ltd., Lucas Digital Ltd. and LucasArt Entertainment Co.
Marquette Medical Systems, Inc.
Marriott International
Mass Mutual
Mattel, Inc.
MBNA America Bank, N.A.
Mentor Graphics Corporation
Merck & Co., Inc.*
Merrill Lynch & Co. Inc.
Millipore Corporation
J. P. Morgan
Motorola, Inc.
NationsBank Corporation*
Neuville Industries, Inc.
Nike, Inc.
Northern Trust Corporation
Owens Corning
Patagonia, Inc.
Plante & Morgan, LLP
Price Waterhouse
The Procter & Gamble Company
Promega Corporation

Resources

Quad/Graphics
Rex Healthcare, Inc.
Ridgeview, Inc.
Rockwell International
  Corporation
The St. Paul Companies
St. Petersburg Times
Salomon Brothers, Inc.
Salt River Project
Sara Lee Corporation
SAS Institute, Inc.*
The Seattle Times
Sequent Computer
  Systems, Inc.
Texas Instruments,
  Incorporated

3M
Tom's of Maine, Inc.
TRW Inc.
Universal Studios, Inc.
Union Life Insurance Co.
  of America
United Services
  Automobile Assoc.
University of Pittsburgh
  Medical Ctr.
USA Group, Inc.
VCW, Inc.
Wearguard
Xerox Corporation*

*Ranked among top 10

Managing Work & Family, Inc.
Bonnie Michaels, President
912 Crain St.
Evanston, IL 60202
Phone: (847) 864-0916
Fax: (847) 475-2021

A work-life consulting and training firm that specializes in conducting needs assessments, manager/employee training, flex pilots, Work-Life Balance Retreats, and Work-Life Training and Licensing programs.

Catalyst
250 Park Avenue South
New York, NY 10003-1459
Phone: (212) 514-7600

A nonprofit research program devoted to developing leadership in women. Focuses on women in the workplace, parental leave policies, flexible benefits, concerns of dual-career families, corporate child care, work-family issues, and flexible work arrangements.

Marketplace Ministries
Gil or Art Stricklin
12900 Preston Road, Suite 1215
Dallas, TX 75230

RESOURCES

Phone: (800) 775-7657; (972) 385-7657
Fax: (972) 385-7307
Web site: http://www.marketplaceministries.com

Since 1984, Marketplace Ministries has offered corporations a unique proactive Employee Assistance Program. Applying a distinctive approach that emphasizes the total person, Marketplace Ministries enables employers to care for the spiritual, social, and emotional needs of their employees. Professionally trained chaplains possess secular work experience as well as strong educational and ministry backgrounds. The staff is culturally diverse and nondenominational. Marketplace Ministries serves individuals of all religious faith preferences, or those with none.

National Institute of Business and Industrial Chaplains
Worklife Institute Consulting
2650 Foundation View Dr.
Houston, TX 77057
Phone: (713) 266-2456
E-mail: nibic@aol.com
Web site: http://www.ncda.org

Index

INDEX

Index

INDEX

About the Authors

Connie Glaser and Barbara Smalley are experts on women in the workplace and have been collaborating for over ten years. Their first book, *More Power to You: How Women Can Communicate Their Way to Success,* has gained international status and been published in over eight languages, including Chinese, Bulgarian, and Hebrew.

Their second book, *Swim with the Dolphins: How Women Can Succeed in Corporate America on Their Own Terms,* quickly established itself as a best-selling business book for women. Providing a "navigational map for the new corporate waters," the book has helped thousands of women in breaking the glass ceiling.

When Money Isn't Enough is their third book to chronicle the changing role of women in the workplace today and to serve as an inspiration for women becoming successful on their *own* terms.

When Money Isn't Enough clearly solidifies Glaser and Smalley's reputation as being among the most influential writers dealing with women in the workplace today.

Connie Glaser is a dynamic and inspiring speaker. She is available for keynote presentations based on *When Money Isn't Enough* or other issues related to women in business. For more information, please call: (770) 804-9290 or (706) 613-7237.

Connie Glaser is one of the country's leading authorities on women in business. A sought-after guest on TV and radio talk shows, she has been featured on *The Today Show, Leeza, Bloomberg News,* CNN and CNBC.

A nationally recognized speaker and consultant, her clients include Xerox, AT&T, Deloitte & Touche, Time Warner, and the U.S. Navy. With a master's degree from the University of Michigan, she has served as a faculty member for the International Management Council and the American Institute of Banking.

Connie was recently named to the World Who's Who of Women. She lives in Atlanta with her husband and two children.

BARBARA SMALLEY has been a successful freelance writer for nearly twenty years. Her specialty is writing for and about women, and she has published more than three hundred articles. Her byline has appeared in national magazines such as *McCall's, Redbook, Cosmopolitan, New Woman, Woman's Day, Woman's World,* and *Reader's Digest.*

Recently Barbara was a recipient of the prestigious ATHENA Award, an international award that recognizes women who selflessly give of their time and talents to help other women reach their goals. She lives in Athens, Georgia, with her husband and their two children.

WON'T YOU SHARE *YOUR* STORY WITH US?

This book owes a true debt of gratitude to the courageous and inspiring women whose stories we've told in these pages. We'd love to hear from you, as well.

If you have a story (your own or someone else's) that you feel belongs in a sequel to this book, please send it to us.

When Money Isn't Enough
740 Old Campus Trail
Atlanta, GA 30328

FAX: (770) 804-0318

e-mail: cglaser1@aol.com or bssmalley@aol.com

We will make sure that you are acknowledged and credited for your contribution.

Thank you!